40

GREAT
RAIL-TRAILS

in New York and
New England

by Karen-Lee ̀

◆◆◆

RAILS-TO-TRAILS CONSERVANCY
SATURN CORPORATION

Contents

Acknowledgments v

Foreword vii

Introduction 1

How to Use Rail-Trails 7

How to Use This Book 9

New York 15

   1. Cayuga County Trail 16
   2. Dryden Lake Park Trail 21
   3. Erie Canal Heritage Trail... 25
   4. Erie Canal Trail 36
   5. Glens Falls Feeder Canal Trail 41
   6. Mohawk-Hudson Bikeway...................................... 47
   7. North County Trailway 57
   8. Old Erie Canal State Park 63
   9. Old Erie Canal Towpath Trail 70
  10. Old Putnam Trail 77
  11. Oswego County Recreation Trail 83
  12. Outlet Trail 88
  13. Rochester, Syracuse & Eastern Trail 95
  14. Sullivan County Trail 99
  15. Wallkill Valley Rail Trail 103
  16. Warren County Bikeway.. 109

Connecticut 113

  17. Airline State Park Trail (South) 114
  18. Farmington Canal Linear State Park Trail............. 120
  19. Hop River State Park Trail 125
  20. Larkin Bridle Path... 133

Rhode Island 139

  21. East Bay Bicycle Path 140

Massachusetts 149

  22. Cape Cod Rail Trail 150
  23. Falmouth Shining Sea Trail 156
  24. Minuteman Bikeway 161
  25. Northampton Bikeway 167
  26. Norwottuck Rail Trail 171
  27. Southwest Corridor Park 176

Vermont 185

  28. Alburg Recreational Rail-Trail 186
  29. Burlington Waterfront Bikeway 191
  30. Central Vermont Rail Trail 196
  31. Delaware and Hudson Rail Trail (North) 203
  32. Delaware and Hudson Rail Trail (South) 209
  33. Montpelier and Wells River Trail 213

New Hampshire 219

  34. Mason Railroad Trail 220
  35. Rockingham Recreational Trail 226
  36. Sugar River Trail 231

Maine 237

  37. Jay to Farmington Trail 238
  38. Solon to Bingham Trail 245
  39. South Portland Greenbelt 249
  40. Woodabogan Trail 253

Saturn Retailers 259

Rails-to-Trails Conservancy Membership and Merchandise 263

About the Author 267

Acknowledgments

This book, the third in the "Great Rail-Trail" series, resulted from the extraordinary partnership between Rails-to-Trails Conservancy, Saturn Corporation, Hearst Magazines and Hal Riney & Partners. I am grateful to many people who continue to make the relationship possible.

From Saturn, thanks to Joe Kennedy, Vice President, Sales, Service and Marketing; John Orth, Director of Consumer Marketing; Mary Ellen Miller, National Advertising Manager; and Dianne Romanelli, Advertising Coordinator.

From Hearst, thanks to Mark E. Goldschmidt, Vice President Marketing and Sales; and Bridget Zukas, *Cosmopolitan* Detroit Manager.

From Hal Riney and Partners, thanks to Ellen Kiyomizu, Vice President, Associate Media Director; Doris Mitsch, Associate Creative Director, Interactive; Cathy Murray, Media Planner; and Elisha Moore, Assistant Account Executive.

Thanks also go to Lisa McGimsey White and Bruce E. White of White & White, Inc., for helping us launch the partnership.

Many other people also deserve recognition for their roles in this book.

Thanks to RTC President David Burwell for providing me with many opportunities over the years, and especially the chance to write another guidebook in the "Great Rail-Trail" series.

Sharon Benjamin, Rails-to-Trails Conservancy's Vice President for Marketing, has been a constant source of strength and support since the book series was launched three years ago. Her faith in my work continues to motivate me with every new venture.

I also want to recognize two special people who made it possible for me to finish this book under tight deadlines: Caroline Baker and April Moore. Caroline, who researched and wrote the East Bay Bicycle Path text, worked tirelessly to fact-check every trail description in the book and still found time to edit a significant portion of the manuscript. April also assisted with the edit and always managed to provide words of encouragement in the process.

While Mark Wood created all of the maps in this book, his most important contribution was his unwavering support of the project and his ability to make me laugh—even at the most stressful moments.

As always, Sally James of Cutting Edge Graphics went above and beyond the role of a graphic designer. She took an interest in the project long before the design phase, always offering friendly advice and innovative design solutions. And, she managed to make the entire production process seem easy. Judy Lutts, also of Cutting Edge, should be recognized for meticulously labeling all of the maps in the book.

Thanks also to a couple of people who contributed to the writing of this book. Boston-area writer Paul Angiolillo researched and wrote the Rockingham Recreational Trail and the Sugar River Trail (both in New Hampshire), as well as the Southwest Corridor Park in Massachusetts. Frances Dumas, of Penn Yan, New York, contributed all of the information used in the Outlet Trail description.

A few hard-working trail advocates deserve special acknowledgment for their hospitality in leading me on trail tours or providing me with much-needed transportation: Alan McClennen, Jr., Minuteman Bikeway; Gary Salmon and Lisa Thornton, Delaware and Hudson Trail; Dave and Laurel Bissett, Mohawk-Hudson Bikeway and Erie Canal Trail; Dan Poitras, Cape Cod Rail Trail; Roland Bahret, Wallkill Valley Rail Trail; and Patrick Beland, Warren County Bikeway and Glens Falls Feeder Canal.

Finally, I would like to thank all of the trail managers in the book for answering questions and providing additional information about the wonderful rail-trails selected for this book.

Karen-Lee Ryan
March, 1996

Foreword

By now, you've probably noticed the Saturn name on the cover of this book. And, if you have, you may be asking a very logical question: why would a car company want to sponsor a guide to a network of "roads" where you can't even drive?

Well, at Saturn, we feel very lucky to live and work in such a beautiful country. And, while we certainly want you to enjoy our cars, we also want you to be able to leave them in the garage now and then.

Which brings us to the subject of this book.

Before cars became our main mode of transportation, cities, towns, parks and forests all across America were connected by the most expansive railway system in the world. Nowadays, thousands of miles of rail corridors are abandoned every year—thousands of miles that pass through some of America's most amazing scenery and interesting places to visit. Fortunately, many of these empty railroad corridors are being converted to a different kind of transportation system.

Rail-trails are not only a beautiful way of preserving an important part of our country's history, they're also ideal for all kinds of sporting and outdoor activities, from walking to bicycling to cross-country skiing.

So we hope you'll take the time to explore a few of the rail-trails in this book—whether it's just for a little fresh air and exercise, to do some sightseeing or simply to get from point A to point B without using a drop of gasoline.

Who knows? Maybe you'll even be inspired to help preserve more rail-trails—in which case, Rails-to-Trails Conservancy would be delighted to hear from you.

In the meantime, let's hit the trail.

From the Saturn Team

Introduction

Welcome to an American adventure! Within these pages, you will find 40 unique experiences on America's fastest growing network of pathways to adventure: rail-trails.

Across the country, thousands of miles of former railroad corridors have been converted to trails for recreation, transportation and open space preservation. Whether you are a bicyclist, a walker, an equestrian, a wheelchair user, a cross-country skier, an in-line skater or an outdoor enthusiast, rail-trails are for you!

Rail-trails traverse every conceivable environment from urban to suburban to rural, passing through farmland, river valleys, wetlands, residential areas, forests and lake shores. In metropolitan areas, rail-trails serve as linear parks that provide a respite from the hustle and bustle of everyday life. In rural areas, they run through some of the most scenic and pristine landscapes America has to offer.

New York and New England play a key role in the rails-to-trails movement. New York is among the nation's top 10 rail-trail states with 34 trails totaling 241 miles, with an additional 60 rail-trail projects underway. The State of New York also is developing a 524-mile Statewide Canalway Trail System, utilizing portions of existing canals, former canals and railroad corridors. Open segments of this phenomenal trail system are included in this book.

New England boasts 76 rail-trails totaling nearing 700 miles, and more than 100 new projects are in the works. While New Hampshire has the most rail-trails of any New England state, many of them are short (3.5 miles average) and are located on National Forest Service land. Maine, on the other hand, is home to 8 rail-trails that total nearly 225 miles, making its average trail length 28 miles. Connecticut offers 12 trails totaling 115 miles while Massachusetts has 9 trails totaling 117 miles and Vermont has 8 trails totaling more than 90 miles. The region's smallest state, Rhode Island, has developed 4 rail-trails totaling 21 miles.

The trails selected for *40 Great Rail-Trails in New York and New England* offer surprising diversity and intriguing experiences for any trail user. New and exciting places await you on these trails. You can travel the route taken by Paul Revere on his famous midnight ride, explore the stunning National Seashore beaches of Cape Cod, venture through two covered bridges, enjoy breathtaking views of the Adirondack Mountains, view restored lift locks along refurbished canals and cross a bridge that spans more than a half-mile. These 40 great rail-trails will lead you to these places and many more.

History of the Rail-Trail Movement

In 1916, the United States was home to the world's most extensive railroad transportation network, with virtually every community connected together by routes of steel. At the pinnacle of the railroading era, nearly 300,000 miles of track spanned the nation—a network six times larger than today's interstate highway system.

Now, *less than half* of that original railroad network exists. Cars, trucks, buses and airplanes have led to the rapid decline of the railroad industry, which continues to abandon more than 2,000 miles of track every year.

The concept of preserving these valuable corridors and converting them into multi-use public trails began in the Midwest, where railroad abandonments were most widespread. Once the tracks came out, people naturally started using the corridors for walking and hiking while exploring railroad relics ranging from train stations and mills to bridges and tunnels.

While many people agreed with this great new concept, the reality of actually converting abandoned railroad corridors into public trails was a much greater challenge. From the late 1960s until the early 1980s, many rail-trail efforts failed as corridors were lost to development, sold to the highest bidder or broken up into many pieces.

In 1983, Congress enacted an amendment to the National Trails System Act directing the Interstate Commerce Commission to allow about-to-be abandoned railroad lines to be "railbanked," or set aside for future transportation use while being used as trails in the interim. In essence, this law preempts rail corridor abandonment, keeping the corridors intact for trail use and any possible future uses.

This powerful new piece of legislation made it easier for agencies and organizations to acquire rail corridors for trails, but many projects still failed because of short deadlines, lack of information and local opposition to trails.

In 1986, Rails-to-Trails Conservancy (RTC) formed to provide a national voice for the creation of rail-trails. RTC quickly developed a strategy to preserve the largest amount of rail corridor in the shortest period of time: a national advocacy program to defend the new railbanking law in the courts and in Congress, coupled with a direct project assistance program to help public agencies and local rail-trail groups overcome the challenges of converting a rail into a trail.

The strategy is working! In 1986, Rails-to-Trails Conservancy knew of only 75 rail-trails and 90 projects in the works. Today, there are more than 750 rail-trails and an additional 900 projects underway. The Rails-to-Trails Conservancy vision of creating an interconnected network of trails across the country is becoming a reality.

The thriving rails-to-trails movement has created more than 7,700 miles of public trails for a wide range of users. And, in 1995, these rail-trails were used more than 90 million times. People all across the country are now realizing the incredible benefits of rail-trails.

Benefits of Rail-Trails

Rail-trails are flat or have gentle grades, making them perfect for multiple users, ranging from walkers and bicyclists to in-line skaters and people with disabilities. In snowy climates, they are perfect for cross-country skiing, snowmobiling and other snow activities. And, because of their length, they offer numerous access points.

In urban areas, rail-trails act as linear greenways through developed areas, efficiently providing much-needed recreation space while also serving as utilitarian transportation corridors. They link neighborhoods and workplaces and connect congested areas to open spaces. In many cities and suburbs, rail-trails are used for commuting to work, school and shopping.

In rural areas, rail-trails can provide a significant stimulus to local economies. People who use trails often spend money on food, beverages, camping, hotels, bed-and-breakfasts, bicycle rentals, souvenirs and other items. Studies have shown that trail users have generated as much as $1.25 million annually for the towns through which a trail passes.

Rail-trails preserve historic structures, such as train stations, bridges, tunnels, mills, factories and canals. These structures preserve an important piece of history and enhance the trail experience.

Wildlife viewing can also enhance the trail experience, and rail-trails are home to birds, plants, wetlands and a variety of small and large mammals. Many rail-trails serve as plant and animal conservation corridors, and, in some cases, endangered species are located along the route.

Recreation, transportation, historic preservation, economic revitalization, open space conservation and wildlife preservation—these are just some of the many benefits of rail-trails and the reasons why people love them.

How to Get Involved

If you enjoy rail-trails, join the movement to save abandoned rail corridors and to create more trails across the country. Donating even a small amount of your time can help get more trails on the ground.

◆ If you only have an hour, write a letter to your city, county or state elected official in favor of pro rail-trail legislation. You could also write a letter to the editor of your local newspaper praising a trail or trail project. Or, you could attend a public hearing to voice your support for a local trail, or send a letter to a friend sharing the special qualities of rail-trails.

◆ If you have a day, volunteer to plant flowers or trees along an existing trail or spend several hours helping out with a cleanup on a nearby rail-trail project. Or, lead a hike along an abandoned corridor with your friends.

◆ If you have several hours a month, become an active member in a trail effort in your area. Many groups host trail events, undertake fundraising campaigns, publish brochures and newsletters and carry out other activities to promote a trail or project. Virtually all of these efforts are completed by volunteers, and they are always looking for another helping hand.

Whatever your time allows, get involved! The success of a community's rail-trail depends upon the level of citizen participation. Rails-to-Trails Conservancy can put you in touch with a local group in your area. And, if you want to keep up on and support the movement nationally, join Rails-to-Trails Conservancy. You will get discounts on all RTC publications and merchandise, and you will be supporting the largest national trails organization in the United States. To become a member, use the order form at the back of this book.

How to Use Rail-Trails

By design, rail-trails accommodate a variety of trail users. While this is generally one of the many benefits of rail-trails, it also can lead to occasional conflicts among trail users. Everyone should take responsibility to ensure trail safety by following a few simple trail etiquette guidelines.

One of the most basic etiquette rules is, "Wheels yield to heels." The figure below indicates the correct protocol for yielding right-of-way. Bicyclists (and in-line skaters) yield to other users; pedestrians yield to equestrians.

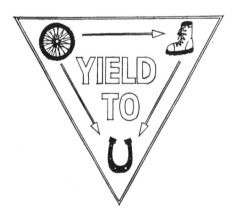

Generally, this means that you need to warn users (to whom you are yielding) of your presence. If, as a bicyclist, you fail to warn a walker that you are about to pass, the walker could step in front you, causing an accident that could have been prevented. Similarly, it is best to slow down and warn an equestrian of your presence. A horse can be startled by a bicycle, so make verbal contact with the rider and be sure it is safe to pass.

Here are some other guidelines you should follow to promote trail safety:

◆ Obey all trail-use rules posted at trailheads.

◆ Stay to the right except when passing.

◆ Pass slower traffic on their left; yield to oncoming traffic when passing.

◆ Give a clear warning signal when passing; for example, call out, "Passing on your left."

◆ Always look ahead and behind when passing.

◆ Travel at a reasonable speed.

◆ Keep pets on a leash.

◆ Do not trespass on private property.

◆ Move off the trail surface when stopped to allow others to pass.

◆ Yield to other trail users when entering and crossing the trail.

◆ Do not disturb any wildlife.

How to Use This Book

At the beginning of each state, you will find a map showing the general location of each rail-trail listed in that state. The text description of every rail-trail begins with the following information:

Trail Name: The official name of the rail-trail is stated here.

Endpoints: This heading lists the endpoints for the entire trail, usually identified by a municipality or a nearby geographical point.

Location: The county or counties through which the trail passes are stated here.

Length: This indicates the length of the trail, including how many miles currently are open, and for those trails that are built partially on abandoned corridors, the number of miles actually on the rail line.

Surface: The materials that make up the surface of the rail-trail vary from trail to trail, and this heading describes each trail's surface, which ranges from asphalt and crushed stone to the significantly more rugged original railroad ballast.

Contact: The name, address and telephone number of each trail's manager are listed here. The selected contacts generally are responsible for managing the trail and can provide additional information about the trail and its condition.

Legend

In addition, every trail has a series of icons depicting uses allowed on the trail.

 walking, hiking, running

in-line skating and roller-skating

bicycling

fishing access

mountain bikes recommended

cross-country skiing

horseback riding

snowmobiling

wheelchair access

all-terrain vehicles

Uses permitted on individual trails are based on trail surfaces and are determined solely by trail managers. Rails-to-Trails Conservancy has no control over which uses are permitted and prohibited.

Wheelchair access is indicated for hard-surface trails. All trails that allow bicycling also allow mountain bicycling, but only on the trail surface—not in surrounding open areas. Trails that only list the mountain bicycling symbol have rougher terrains that are not suitable for road bikes. The all-terrain vehicle symbol generally does not include motorcycles and minibikes.

Map Legend

●	Trail endpoints	– – –	County borders
▬	Rail-Trail	— —	State borders
P	Parking	(95)	Interstate highway
◆	Point of interest	(301)	U.S. highway
⋯⋯⋯	Active railroad track	(213)	State Route

Rail-Trail Safety

The author of this book has made every effort to ensure the accuracy of the information included here, however trails and their conditions can change at any time. It is your responsibility to ensure your own safety and exercise caution while using rail-trails. This includes knowing the limits of your own abilities and wearing a helmet when bicycling.

If you find inaccurate information or substantially different conditions, please send a letter detailing your findings to: Publications Department, Rails-to-Trails Conservancy, 1400 Sixteenth Street, NW, Washington, DC 20036.

THE 40 GREAT RAIL-TRAILS OF NEW YORK AND NEW ENGLAND

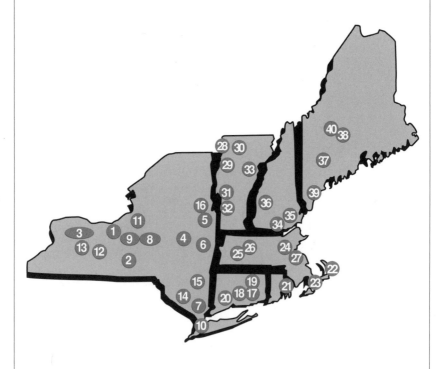

New York

1. Cayuga County Trail
2. Dryden Lake Park Trail
3. Erie Canal Heritage Trail
4. Erie Canal Trail
5. Glens Falls Feeder Canal Trail
6. Mohawk-Hudson Bikeway
7. North County Trailway
8. Old Erie Canal State Park
9. Old Erie Canal Towpath Trail
10. Old Putnam Trail
11. Oswego County Recreation Trail
12. Outlet Trail
13. Rochester, Syracuse & Eastern Trail
14. Sullivan County Rail Trail
15. Wallkill Valley Rail Trail
16. Warren County Bikeway

Connecticut

17. Airline State Park Trail (South)
18. Farmington Canal Linear State Park Trail
19. Hop River State Park Trail
20. Larkin Bridle Path

Rhode Island

21. East Bay Bicycle Path

Massachusetts

22. Cape Cod Rail Trail
23. Falmouth Shining Sea Trail
24. Minuteman Bikeway
25. Northampton Bikeway
26. Norwottuck Rail-Trail
27. Southwest Corridor Park

Vermont

28. Alburg Recreational Rail-Trail
29. Burlington Waterfront Bikeway
30. Central Vermont Rail Trail
31. Delaware and Hudson Rail Trail (North)
32. Delaware and Hudson Rail Trail (South)
33. Montpelier and Wells River Trail

New Hampshire

34. Mason Railroad Trail
35. Rockingham Recreational Trail
36. Sugar River Trail

Maine

37. Jay to Farmington Trail
38. Solon to Bingham Trail
39. South Portland Greenbelt
40. Woodabogan Trail

New York's Great Rail-Trails

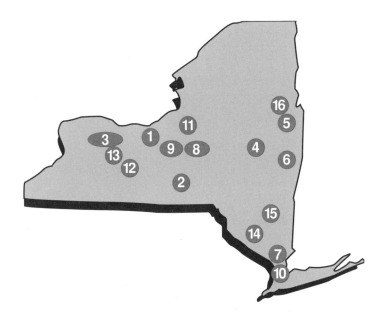

1. Cayuga County Trail
2. Dryden Lake Park Trail
3. Erie Canal Heritage Trail
4. Erie Canal Trail
5. Glens Falls Feeder Canal Trail
6. Mohawk-Hudson Bikeway
7. North County Trailway
8. Old Erie Canal State Park
9. Old Erie Canal Towpath Trail
10. Old Putnam Trail
11. Oswego County Recreation Trail
12. Outlet Trail
13. Rochester, Syracuse & Eastern Trail
14. Sullivan County Trail
15. Wallkill Valley Rail Trail
16. Warren County Bikeway

The Cayuga County Trail is lightly wooded near the town of Fair Haven.

1. Cayuga County Trail

Endpoints: Fair Haven to Cato

Location: Cayuga County

Length: 14 miles

Surface: Grass, dirt and cinder

Uses:

Contact: Tom Higgins, County Planner
Cayuga County Planning Board
160 Genessee Street
Auburn, NY 13021-1276
315-253-1276

◆◆◆

Beginning near the shores of Lake Ontario, the Cayuga County Trail travels through the rural countryside of New York's Finger Lakes region. If you are looking for quiet serenity, you will find it on the Cayuga County Trail.

In an area heavily populated by snowmobilers, it comes as no surprise that this trail was opened in 1974 to serve as a county snowmobiling route (in the context of a larger county recreation plan). It has become a popular multi-use trail over the years, and it is now used by nearly as many walkers during warm months as snowmobilers during snowy months.

The corridor was built by Lehigh Valley Railroad and transported coal and other products from Pennsylvania to the route's terminus at Lake Ontario in Fair Haven. From there, the freight was loaded onto steamships headed for Canada and other destinations. Today, many campers at nearby Fair Haven Beach State Park venture out of the park to enjoy the trail.

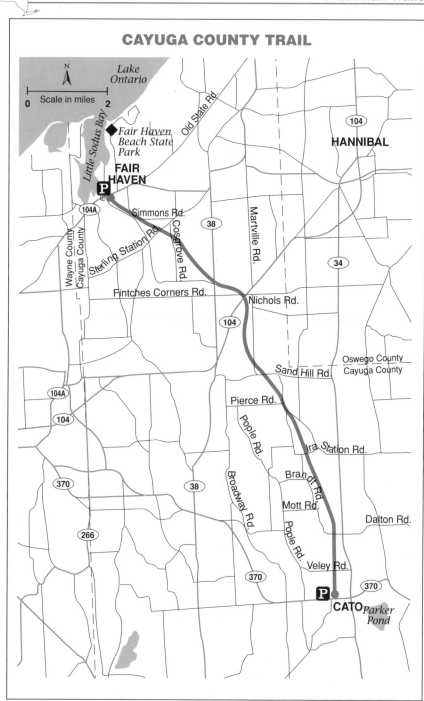

CAYUGA COUNTY TRAIL

N

Lake Ontario

Scale in miles
0   2

Little Sodus Bay

◆ Fair Haven Beach State Park

Old State Rd.

104

HANNIBAL

FAIR HAVEN

P

104A

Simmons Rd.

Sterling Station Rd.

Cosgrove Rd.

38

Martville Rd.

34

Wayne County
Cayuga County

Fintches Corners Rd.

Nichols Rd.

104

Sand Hill Rd.

Oswego County
Cayuga County

104A

Pierce Rd.

104

Pople Rd.

Ira Station Rd.

370

38

Broadway Rd.

Brandt Rd.

Mott Rd.

Dalton Rd.

266

Pople Rd.

Veley Rd.

370

P **CATO** Parker Pond

Karen-Lee Ryan

The surroundings of the Cayuga County Trail are decidedly rural.

The 865-acre Fair Haven State Park is located about 15 miles southwest of Oswego. If you don't want to stay at one of the 200 campsites or three dozen cabins, you can still spend time enjoying the park's other amenities: a large beach and swimming area with seasonal concessions, hiking trails, picnic tables, boat rentals, rest rooms with hot showers and a playground. From Route 104A, the trail parking lot is located on the left 0.3 miles south of the access road to Fair Haven Beach State Park.

Starting on the trail at the southern edge of Fair Haven, you feel pleasantly isolated. While dense vegetation lines the route, the trail corridor itself is initially quite open. By the time you cross Sterling Station Road in less than 2 miles, sumac, beech, maple and aspen trees shroud the corridor. The Cayuga County Trail continues straight at Sterling Station Road, although another former railroad corridor, veers away from the route. This is the recently opened Hojack Trail, which currently stretches 8 miles between Red Creek and Hannibal.

In the next few miles, you pass by a number of farms, as the corridor gets progressively more rural. Be aware that the only towns along this trail are located at the endpoints. About 3.5 miles from Fair Haven, you cross Route 38 at grade. In less than a mile, you cross the even busier Route 104 at grade before reaching a narrow bridge. Here, you get scenic views of Sterling Creek before heading back into the woods, where the trail gradually widens into a two-track. The surroundings remain pleasantly wooded, with maple trees dominating the perimeter for the next several miles.

Where the trail crosses Ira Station Road (near its intersection with Follett Road), the trail begins veering more directly south on its way to Cato, which is now about 5 miles away. You remain in a canopy of trees, and, if it is summertime, the route will be lined with a mix of ferns and wildflowers.

The trail actually ends at West Main Street (Route 370) in Cato, the economic center of Cayuga County. While this town is agriculturally oriented, you will find several shops and restaurants, as well as an old historic hotel that once catered to railroad employees.

2. Dryden Lake Park Trail

Endpoints: Dryden

Location: Tompkins County

Length: 3.3 miles (will be 5.3 miles when complete)

Surface: Original ballast

Uses:

Contact: Jim Shugg, Supervisor
Town of Dryden
65 East Main Street
Dryden, NY 13053
607-844-8619

◆◆◆

onsidered one of the best bird watching sites in the entire Finger Lakes Region of New York, Dryden Lake is an off-the-beaten-path destination. And the 3.3-mile Dryden Lake Park Trail offers an intimate look at the lake and the wetlands that surround it.

The town of Dryden, population 1,908, is located 12 miles southwest of Cortland via State Route 13 (Exit 11 from Interstate 81). Parking for the trail is available at the municipal parking lot in downtown Dryden and at the lake. From the downtown parking lot, take a right on George Street and a left on Mill Street, where you will soon see a railroad trestle on your right. The northern end of the trail ends beyond the trestle, just shy of Route 13, which is Main Street through Dryden. Turn left onto the trail to head toward Dryden Lake.

A half-mile from the parking lot, you see the first of several interpretive signs and benches located at half-mile intervals along

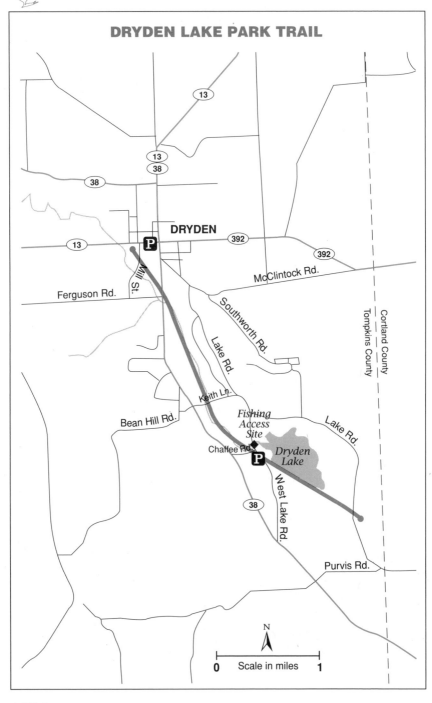

DRYDEN LAKE PARK TRAIL

13

13
38

38

DRYDEN

P

13   392

392

McClintock Rd.

Ferguson Rd.   Mill St.

Southworth Rd.

Cortland County
Tompkins County

Lake Rd.

Keith Ln.

Bean Hill Rd.   *Fishing
Access
Site*

Chaffee Rd.   *Dryden
Lake*   Lake Rd.

P

38   West Lake Rd.

Purvis Rd.

N

0   Scale in miles   1

the trail. The first sign describes an old Borden Milk plant that once sat adjacent to the rail corridor. Built in 1905, the collection and bottling plant served local dairy farmers until 1960.

Soon you cross State Route 38 at grade and then travel over a creek on a short wooden bridge. A sign at the 1-mile mark describing the corridor's wildlife is particularly helpful because you are paralleling a designated wetland area known as Dryden Sedge Meadow. The wetlands, which attract ospreys, warblers, swallows and dozens of other bird species, line your right side, while a stream trickles on the left. The setting is quite serene; you may want to take some time to relax and enjoy the lovely scenery.

You pass another bench at the 1.5-mile mark, before crossing over another wooden bridge. Next, you cross Keith Road at grade before arriving at the 2-mile mark and another interpretive sign. This one describes the area's extensive beaver activity, which includes a dam that is 80-yards wide.

In less than a half-mile, you arrive at the trail's namesake, Dryden Lake. This beautiful body of water was formed by a

The Dryden Lake Fishing Access Site offers some of the best lake views.

glacial depression, and a recent archaeological dig revealed that native Americans had inhabited this area for nearly 3,000 years and had used the lake as their prime hunting and fishing area. You will see lake views from the Dryden Lake Fishing Access Site, where rest rooms and parking are located.

At the 2.5-mile mark, a sign describes another industry that formed part of the route's history. During the railroad's heyday, the lake was used to harvest ice, and the ice houses that once stored the ice were located in the vicinity of the trail's 2.5-mile mark.

More opportunities for birding await along the shores of Lake Dryden. Great blue and little green herons are prevalent in the area. You might also catch a glimpse of the area's wide variety of ducks, including mergansers, buffleheads, mallards and widgeons.

The trail ends soon after the end of the lake, near the Tompkins County line. By the end of 1996, local authorities hope to extend the trail another 2 miles to Willow Crossing in Cortland County.

3. Erie Canal Heritage Trail

Endpoints: Palmyra to Lockport

Location: Wayne, Monroe, Orleans and Niagara Counties

Length: 85 miles

Surface: Primarily crushed stone, with some sections of asphalt or dirt

Uses:

 on certain sections

Contact: John DiMurra, Canalway Project Manager
New York State Thruway Authority
200 Southern Boulevard
Albany, NY 12209
514-436-3034

If you are looking for a multi-day trail excursion that combines a mix of rural countrysides, small town charm and urban diversity, head to the Erie Canal Heritage Trail. The trail spans nearly 100 miles of western New York, with Rochester near its mid-point. And, it parallels one of New York's most intriguing and historically significant waterways: the Erie Canal.

Construction of the original 363-mile Erie Canal began in 1817 and by 1825 it spanned the entire state. As traffic increased, the need arose to expand the canal. Construction of the Enlarged Erie Canal began in 1841 and continued through much of the 1800s. In 1905, New York authorized the development of a comprehensive New York State Barge Canal system. The plan incorporated portions of the Enlarged Erie Canal (and called for moving remaining sections into the Mohawk and Seneca Rivers), with three other

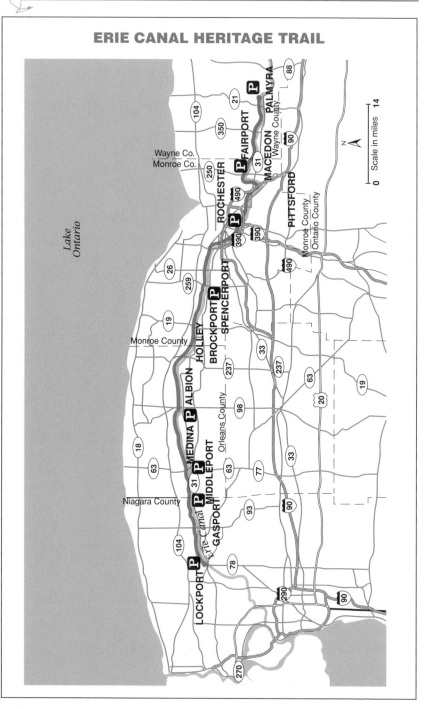

ERIE CANAL HERITAGE TRAIL

canals: the Champlain, the Oswego and the Cayuga and Seneca. The New York State Barge Canal System remains fully navigable today.

The latest chapter in the history of this unique resource is a plan that calls for developing a 524-mile statewide recreational trail system utilizing portions of existing canals, former canals and railroad corridors. It is called the Statewide Canalway Trail System, and this 85-mile segment from Palmyra to Lockport is the longest open section of the system.

A trip on any segment of the Erie Canal Heritage Trail will convince you that New York State is developing one of the most spectacular interconnected trail systems in the nation. The State expects to release a new map of the system in spring 1996, including a detailed panel of the Erie Canal Heritage Trail. To request a copy, call 1-800-4 CANAL 4.

Palmyra to Fairport

The section between Palmyra and Fairport currently is the most rugged portion of this 85-mile trail. Plans call for the state to surface the trail with crushed limestone by 1997. The towpath actually continues farther eastward toward Lyons, although that section of trail is not yet developed. If you do opt to travel that way, be prepared for an even more rugged experience than the 10 miles between Palmyra and Fairport.

The best place to begin this eastern end of the trail is Palmyra's Aqueduct Park, located on State Route 31, west of State Route 21, about 5 miles north of Interstate 90 (the New York State Thruway). This sizable park incorporates both the existing Erie Canal and some elements of the old Erie Canal, including an aqueduct. Other features include camp sites, picnic tables, swing sets, rest rooms and extensive parking facilities.

After exploring the park, head west out of Palmyra, traveling on the south bank of the still-in-use Erie Canal. This section of trail closely parallels State Route 31 for the 3 miles into Macedon. The surface is fairly rugged with a mix of dirt and gravel.

As you enter Macedon, you see a Mobil Company chemical plant ahead of you. Before you reach it, turn right onto Quaker Road, cross over the canal, and resume the trip on the north bank

Karen-Lee Ryan

In the southeastern suburbs of Rochester, sections of the Erie Canal Heritage Trail are paved, making it popular with in-line skaters.

of the canal. Soon, you pass Lock 30, and, if you venture back across to the south side of the canal, you can explore historic Lock 61. Built in 1842, this preserved lock is now wedged between the existing canal and the Mobil plant.

Between Macedon and Wayneport, you are closely paralleling several sets of railroad tracks, including an active Conrail line. In this area, the canal is quite wide, with some lake-like areas. Houses often separate you from the canal.

In the small town of Wayneport, the trail cuts close to a long stretch of mobile homes that are tucked next to the canal, which is quite wide at this point. Once you cross into Monroe County, the surface begins to improve. Fairport, where many trail services are available, is located about 4 miles west of the county line.

As you near the town of Fairport, a short stretch of trail doubles as an access road, making for a bumpy ride. The surface turns into asphalt, and you soon pass under Turk Hill Road, signaling your entrance into the Village of Fairport.

Fairport to Spencerport

This section of trail spans the distant suburbs of Rochester and leads into the city limits before easing its way into the rural environs beyond. Many people actually forgo the far eastern section described above and begin the journey on the Erie Canal Heritage Trail in Fairport, where the more developed section of the trail actually begins. On-street parking is available in downtown Fairport, Pittsford and Spencerport, as well as in several parks in the Rochester area.

Continuing east, the trail remains paved for a couple of miles as you wend your way through Fairport. Route 250 doubles as Main Street in this pleasant town, and if you want to take a break, get off the trail here. You can also make an easy on-road connection to a local rail-trail known as the Rochester, Syracuse and Eastern Trail (see page 95).

The 10-mile section between Fairport and Pittsford seems to be the most heavily traveled section of the trail. Many services—including carry-out cafes, full-service restaurants, specialty shops, visitor centers, bike rentals and even canal boat tours—are available just a short distance from the trail. Some retailers even cater to the crowds on the trail corridor.

Between Fairport and Pittsford, the surface turns into a hard-packed crushed limestone. Many sizable homes, often with private boat slips, line the left shore of the canal. On your right, the corridor is densely wooded. You pass under U.S. Route 490 before State Route 96 begins paralleling the trail on the other side of the canal and remains nearby for the next 2 miles. In this same stretch, you are likely to see a variety of tour boats cruising up and down the canal.

You know you are entering the town of Pittsford when the asphalt surface resumes. In the downtown area, you cut under Main Street before passing under a massive steel trestle still used by Conrail. This scene provides a nice juxtaposition of two interconnected historical forms of transportation. Soon, you reach Lock 32, where parking, picnic tables and rest rooms are available. This lock is followed closely by Lock 33, and with a little luck, you may see one of these two lift locks in operation.

The next 10 miles of trail are by far the most urban, as you skirt the southern boundary of Rochester. Despite the fact that highways and other major thoroughfares surround you, you will not experience a single at-grade crossing for the entire urban distance—primarily because the canal existed before this web of roads. The asphalt surface continues throughout this section, which also receives heavy use.

You pass under Interstate 390 twice before it begins paralleling the trail's left side beyond the canal. However, because the canal is sunken down, the highway is less noticeable than you might think. About 4 miles from Lock 33, you enter Genessee Valley Park, the highlight of this densely populated segment.

This massive Olmstead-designed park is centered around the scenic Genessee River. Take some time to explore the park's many amenities, including shelters, picnic tables, a swimming pool, baseball diamonds, soccer fields, an ice rink, rest rooms, a golf course and extensive parking—all surrounded by rolling grassy areas.

On the west side of the Genessee River, the trail crosses over the Erie Canal and resumes on the opposite bank, but it can be

PITTSFORD TRAIL SYSTEM

Settled in 1789, the town of Pittsford has historically been a farming community, producing the nation's largest number of kidney beans for many years. Over the last couple of decades, the town of Pittsford has rapidly become a suburb of Rochester, and in recent years, the town had been losing a half-acre of farmland every day to development. This revelation spurred the formation of a group called Greenbelt, which established the goal of preserving open space throughout the community.

This effort was so successful, that it spawned a related group—the Pittsford Trails Coalition. Its goal is to connect all of the existing open spaces with nearly 40 miles of linear recreation paths. To date, the group has created almost 10 miles of trails, strictly through volunteer effort. While this mileage is not yet continuous, you can get a flavor of the Coalition's accomplishments by taking a short sidetrip from the Erie Canal Heritage Trail. Just east of Lock 32, you find a one-mile sidepath that ends at Lock 62 of the original Erie Canal.

ERIE CANAL HERITAGE TRAIL (DETAIL)

tricky getting there. The park contains three magnificent stone arch bridges across the canal. Pass by the first two that head left off the trail. To get to the third one, you must first cross the Genessee River on a bridge to your right. This one is dedicated to the late Waldo J. Nielsen, a local trails visionary. After crossing the river, you will see the third arched bridge that carries you over the canal and back to the towpath. (You will know it is the correct bridge if it is adjacent to an abandoned railroad bridge.)

As you exit the park, you are in the vicinity of the Rochester International Airport, and you may hear and see some planes. Railroad tracks also dominate the area, and I-390 continues to parallel the trail on the left for another 3 miles. In this section you are actually within the Rochester city limits, where you are likely to see signs of your urban environment, including occasional litter, graffiti and vacant warehouses.

When you cross under I-390 near several large businesses (including a Kodak Distribution Center), you leave the city limits and the trail starts to lose its urban feel surprisingly quickly. In the town of South Greece, you cross to the other side of the canal again near State Route 386 (Elmgrove Road), where parking is available. Looking around, it is hard to imagine that South Greece was a bustling canal town in the 1800s. At that time, a large grocery store, a post office, a school and two doctor's offices were located in this area.

In South Greece, the trail returns to a hard-packed crushed limestone surface. The hardness of the stone trail surface varies from town to town, but asphalt does not resume until you reach Lockport. By the time you reach the small town of Ogden, the setting has changed dramatically, with woods and farmland surrounding the trail.

A large sign across the Route 259 drawbridge marks your arrival into Spencerport, where a few shops and eateries are located. From this point west, every town seems to have one or more fascinating bridges—some look like works of art—that cross

Many historic buildings line the shores of the Erie Canal.

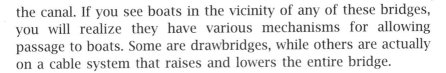

the canal. If you see boats in the vicinity of any of these bridges, you will realize they have various mechanisms for allowing passage to boats. Some are drawbridges, while others are actually on a cable system that raises and lowers the entire bridge.

Spencerport to Lockport

This far western section of the Erie Canal Heritage Trail is dotted with small towns in an otherwise agricultural setting. On-street parking is available in the downtown areas of Brockport, Albion, Medina and Middleport, as well as in several locations in Lockport.

As you head west out of Spencerport, the surface is a bit bumpier. If you want a smoother surface, you can get onto Canal Road, which generally runs parallel to the trail for the 8 miles to Brockport.

The trail gradually undulates while the road remains flat off to the right side. Vegetation is sparse within the canal corridor, although dense woods line the area. You pass by some residences as you make your way into Brockport. During the mid-1800s, this town was famous for production of reapers, which were machines designed to harvest grain.

Brockport is significantly larger than Spencerport, with a mix of shops and restaurants on Main Street. In fact, it is the largest service area for trail users between Rochester and Lockport. It is also about the halfway point of the trail, located more than 40 miles west of Palmyra and nearly 45 miles east of Lockport. As you leave town, you may see a series of brick buildings to your left. These are part of the Brockport Campus of the State University of New York.

You cross into Orleans County before reaching the small town of Holley, where you find a grocery store and two restaurants about 5 miles west of Brockport. This section of trail is lightly used. The placid canal barely moves along your left side, while a mix of hardwoods—including many locust trees—line your right side.

The surroundings for the next 9 miles (to Albion) are generally agricultural. Various crops are grown in the area, including corn, garlic, apples and butternut squash. This section of trail is very lightly traveled, and on many days you are more likely to see a red-tailed hawk than another trail user. If you are looking for a peaceful spot, head to this section of the trail.

You can park on-street or in the municipal lot in the town of Albion, which serves as the County Seat of Orleans County. If you venture off the trail, you can take a look at historic Courthouse Square, which is about a quarter-mile south of the trail via Main Street (State Route 98). A 175-foot spire, stemming from a sandstone Presbyterian Church, demands your attention, while a quick tour through town reveals some other historic structures. A Methodist Church dates back to 1860, a nearby library opened in 1900 and the Greek-Revival Courthouse was built between 1857 and 1858.

Once outside of Albion (turn around to get one last view of the spire), the trail's right side is dominated by corn fields. Farm fields continue to surround the route all the way to Medina, about 10.5 miles west of Albion. This section of trail gets very little use, and the trail is somewhat choppy with grass and weeds occasionally growing through the surface.

About 8 miles west of Albion, the trail and canal actually cross over a street called Culvert Road. It is listed in *Ripley's Believe It Or Not* because it is the only road that passes under the entire Erie Canal. Built in 1823, this tunnel is an intriguing sight along the canal—get off the trail and take a look at it.

You pass a few picnic tables as you make your way into the town of Medina, where the surface suddenly improves. The State laid down a new hard-packed, crushed limestone surface in 1994 from Medina to Lockport, making this one of the smoothest sections of the entire trail.

Paralleling Horan Street as you enter Medina, the trail and canal make a loose, u-shaped curve to make their way around Glenwood Lake. Medina seems to be suffering from loss of industry, although a trip through town exposes some lovely Victorian architecture. State Route 63 is the main road through town, where you will find a couple of restaurants. From here, you are about 3.5 miles from the Niagara County line to the west, 45 miles from Genesee Valley Park in Rochester and more than 65 miles from the trail's eastern end in Palmyra.

The hard-packed crushed stone continues as you make your way into Middleport, just a mile into Niagara County. Parking

Karen-Lee Ryan

The far western end of the Erie Canal Heritage Trail is highly scenic and lightly used.

and a few services are available in this quaint town that seems to attract many recreational boaters along the canal.

You pass a golf course off to your left as you head to tiny Gasport, 5 miles west of Middleport. Equally tiny Orangeport soon follows, and from here you are less than 5 miles from Lockport and the trail's western terminus. Enjoy the quiet serenity of this stretch of path.

You reach a small canalside park in Lockport, and you can see a massive lock ahead of you. The trail ends here, although you can make your way up to the street level and watch boats make their way through Locks 34 and 35 in downtown Lockport.

The Erie Canal is obviously a major attraction in this town, where you can take a short trip on a historic locks walkway or visit the Erie Canal Museum. Or, if you have more time, plan to take the full walking tour of this historic city. The Eastern Niagara Chamber of Commerce, located at 151 West Genessee Street, offers maps and other information about what to do in the Lockport area. For more information, call 716-433-3828.

Karen-Lee Ryan

Putnam's Store, near historic lock #28, has been restored along the Erie Canal Trail.

4. Erie Canal Trail

Endpoints: Fort Hunter (Schoharie Crossing State Historic Site) to Amsterdam

Location: Montgomery County

Length: 8 miles (will be 90 miles when complete)

Surface: Asphalt

Uses:

Contact: Janice Fontanella, Site Manager
Schoharie Crossing State Historic Site
P.O. Box 140
Fort Hunter, NY 12069-7516
(518) 829-7516

◆◆◆

Less than an hour from New York's capital, the well-endowed Schoharie Crossing State Historic Site is an ideal starting point for the newly developed, paved Erie Canal Trail. The Historic Site is an attractive destination for travelers interested in the history of the Erie Canal. The trail highlights the development and growth of the original Erie Canal, the Enlarged Erie Canal and the New York State Barge Canal.

A small section of New York's proposed 524-mile Canalway Trail System, this 8-mile segment known as the Erie Canal Trail will eventually extend 90 miles to connect with the Mohawk-Hudson Bikeway in Rotterdam Junction (see page 47) and the Old Erie Canal State Park in Rome (see page 63). The 8-mile segment that opened in 1992 follows a corridor originally developed by the West Shore Railroad, which was in direct competition with the New York Central Railroad.

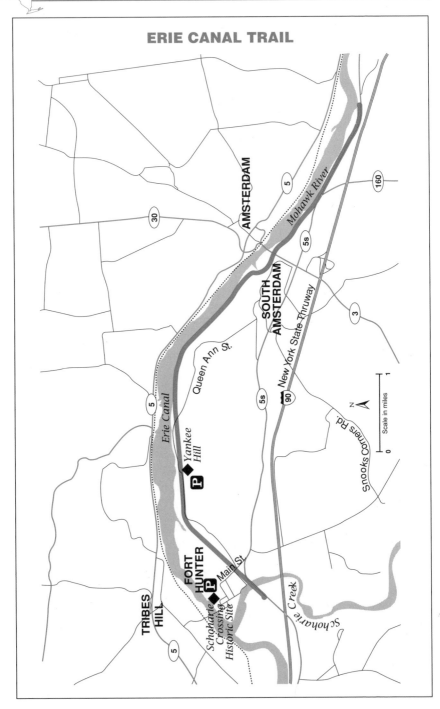

ERIE CANAL TRAIL

To get to Schoharie Crossing State Historic Site from Albany, take Interstate 90 to Exit 27. Turn right onto State Route 30 north, then immediately turn right onto State Route 5S and head west. When you reach Fort Hunter in 4 miles, turn right onto Main Street and cross the trail (you will see a steel trestle). You can park here or turn left onto Railroad Street to reach the Historic Site Visitors Center and a large parking lot on the right. The Center is open Wednesday through Sunday from May 15 to the last Sunday in October. The grounds are open during daylight hours year-round.

Plan to spend some time exploring this historic area, which features several locks from both the original and enlarged canals, as well as 7 of the 14 original arches of the Schoharie Aqueduct. An exhibit in the Visitors Center illustrates the canal's history and its impact on the growth of the Northeast. The Center also provides several brochures, including one that describes a 3-mile walking (or bicycling) tour highlighting the history and natural features of the area. This tour—which follows the dirt canal towpath—is separate from the rail-trail, but can easily be made into a loop on the trail's western end.

The Erie Canal Trail's current western endpoint is on the far side of the railroad trestle you passed as you entered the Historic Site. If you venture across it, you can take in some attractive views of Schoharie Creek flowing into the Mohawk River. Just beyond the trestle, you see that the corridor is thick with vegetation and not passable. Heading back east, the corridor is flat and straight, with sumac dominating the vegetation along this newly developed trail. You will see mileage markers painted on the pavement in half-mile increments.

Beyond the 2-mile mark, you reach Yankee Hill Lock #28, the site of a 220-foot double lock that was expanded in 1889. This inviting grassy area offers dozens of picnic tables, several grills, rest rooms and more parking. Relax and enjoy the views, or take a minute to explore Putnam's Store. Built in the mid-1800s, it was one of 40 stores that served a 14-mile segment of the Erie Canal. This store—carrying such diverse items as medicine, shoes, candy, kerosene and horse collars—operated until 1908.

The vegetation is more abundant beyond Yankee Hill, obscuring views of the Mohawk River off to the left. You are likely to hear at least a couple of trains rumbling on the river's opposite bank. And, depending on the season, you may see a mix of wildflowers along the trail, including goldenrod, purple loosestrife, asters and wild sunflowers. Birds, also abundant in the area, include goldfinches, doves, cardinals and chickadees.

By the 4.5-mile mark, you enter South Amsterdam, where you need to negotiate a couple of dangerous at-grade crossings. At Arch Street, you can see the foundations of a removed bridge, which limit your ability to see oncoming traffic—use caution. You also go under State Route 30 and pass a stone post marked with a "W." This whistle post once signaled train engineers to blow their whistles as they entered town. You soon leave South Amsterdam, quickly reentering the woods.

By mile 6, Route 5S begins paralleling your right side, but because it is raised high above you, it is not very noticeable. If you look to your left, you can see some closed-down factories across the river in Amsterdam. The County Seat of Montgomery County, Amsterdam once was home to a major carpet manufacturing industry.

As you near the eastern end of the trail, Route 5S moves progressively closer to the trail. Just before the 8-mile mark, the trail ends anticlimactically near the state highway. The Mohawk-Hudson Bikeway (see page 47) is only about 7 miles from this point. Plans call for connecting the two trails, but the rail corridor in between cannot be used at this point because it still serves two quarries. As you travel back toward Schoharie Crossing State Historic Site, consider taking the dirt towpath trail from Yankee Hill back to the Visitors Center to see some of the area's other historic sites.

5. Glens Falls Feeder Canal Trail

Endpoints: Glens Falls to Fort Edward

Location: Warren and Washington Counties

Length: 9 miles

Surface: Crushed stone and gravel

Uses:

Contact: John DiMurra, Canalway Project Manager
New York State Thruway Authority
200 Southern Boulevard
Albany, NY 12209
518-436-3034

◆◆◆

Created from two canals and a tiny stretch of rail corridor, the Glens Falls Feeder Canal Trail offers an intriguing mix of industrial heritage contrasted with dense woodlands and striking views of the Hudson River. The Glens Falls Feeder Canal joined the Champlain Canal and served as an integral part of eastern New York's transportation system. And, today they are key links in the 524-mile Statewide Canalway Trail System.

To get to the trail's western end, take Exit 18 from Interstate 87 (Adirondack Northway) and travel east on Corinth Road (County Route 28). In 0.6 miles turn south (right) onto Richardson Street, which turns to the left after a half-mile. Turn right onto Edgewater Place, which ends at Towpath Lane. Parking is available here, where the Glens Falls Feeder Canal meets the Hudson River.

From the parking area, you cross a short footbridge and begin the trail near the shores of the Hudson River. The trail corridor quickly becomes wooded and peaceful. You catch fleeting

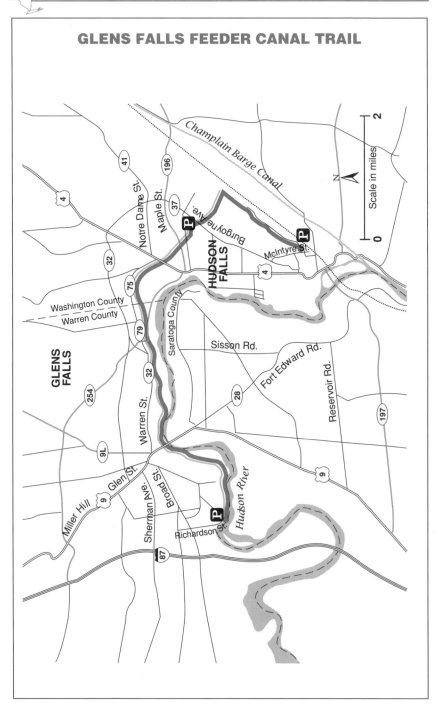

GLENS FALLS FEEDER CANAL TRAIL

Just east of Glens Falls, the trail's surroundings become pleasantly remote.

glimpses of the river to your right, while the Glens Falls Feeder Canal lines your left side.

Beyond the half-mile mark, you can take a quick side trip to Haviland's Cove, a park where you will find rest rooms, a large swimming area and picnic tables in a wooded setting. A right turn onto Bush Street leads directly into the park. Back on the trail, you pick up wonderful views of the Hudson.

In a little more than a mile, you pass a timber-related commercial development, where logs are piled high near the trail corridor. Since the right side of the trail has been cleared to accommodate power lines, you can enjoy excellent views of the Hudson River.

At 2 miles, a large dam in the Hudson and a paper company across the towpath force you to make a 1.2-mile detour through the heart of Glens Falls. At the end of a large parking lot, you need to jog briefly to the left before turning right on Mohican Street. As you cross U.S. Route 9 (Glen Street) and pass the Civic Center, Mohican Street turns into Oakland Avenue. Route 9 crosses the Hudson River and leads to a couple of fast-food restaurants on the other side. Oakland Avenue ends in 0.3 miles at Warren Street, where you turn right. You may want to stop at a museum called the Hyde Collection, which houses paintings, sculpture, furniture and books, some dating back to the 5th century B.C. Continue a half-mile on Warren Street before turning right onto Shermantown Road. Proceed 0.2 miles and pick up the trail on the left.

A series of former locks are an intriguing site along the Glens Falls Feeder Canal Trail.

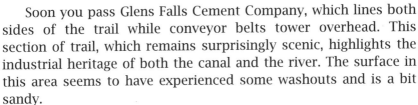

Soon you pass Glens Falls Cement Company, which lines both sides of the trail while conveyor belts tower overhead. This section of trail, which remains surprisingly scenic, highlights the industrial heritage of both the canal and the river. The surface in this area seems to have experienced some washouts and is a bit sandy.

Before the 4-mile mark, you pass under a set of railroad tracks and continue past several more industrial sites. Views of the Hudson River continue on your right, while a busy road parallels the trail on the left. In a half-mile, you enter Washington County near Warren Street. The trail and the canal create a serene setting for the next 2 miles. You quickly feel miles from anywhere as weeping willows dot the canal's edge and mature, graceful maples arch over the trail.

As you cross State Route 196, where it intersects with Lower Feeder Street, you cross the canal and continue along the trail on the opposite bank. Private residences soon surround both sides of the trail and the canal.

In about a half-mile, you cross busy Burgoyne Avenue at grade and arrive at a series of descending locks that now look like a waterfall. The best view of the locks' stonework can be seen from the two bridges that cross the locks. Picnic tables and a couple of grills are nearby. Ahead of you and slightly to the left is a large, grassy hill that was once an active landfill; it has since been converted into a grassy open space. Parking is available in this area, located just beyond the trail's 7-mile point.

The trail doubles as Feeder Tow Road for a half-mile as you descend a relatively steep hill. You also pass several locks in the canal and several bridges that cross it. This descent marks the eastern end of the Glens Falls Feeder Canal where it makes its way to join the original Champlain Canal, which was eventually replaced by the still-in-use Champlain Barge Canal.

When you reach the bottom of the hill, you come to a "T" intersection at the old Champlain Canal. The path to the right is surfaced with crushed stone and continues for nearly 2 miles before ending at Energy Park on McIntyre Street in Fort Edward. On the way, you pass through some farmland (with cows that often hover near the trail) and by a paper plant. If you cross McIntyre Street, you reach McIntyre Park, which has tennis and basketball courts, baseball fields, a swing set, a portable toilet and ample parking. The path that heads to the left at the "T" is not yet developed, but eventually will extend nearly 25 miles as part of the Statewide Canalway Trail System.

6. Mohawk-Hudson Bikeway

Endpoints: Albany to Rotterdam Junction

Location: Albany and Schenectady Counties

Length: 20 miles of a 41-mile trail is on abandoned rail corridor

Surface: Asphalt and crushed stone

Uses: 🚶 🚲 ♿ 🛼 🎣 ⛷️

🛷 on certain sections

Contact: **Albany Section**
Mark King, Senior Natural Resource Planner
Albany County Department of Planning
  and Conservation
112 State Street, Room 1006
Albany, NY 12207-2005
518-447-5660

Colonie Section
James Zambardino, Superintendent
Colonie Parks and Recreation Department
89 Schermerhorn Road
Cohoes, NY 12047-0442
518-783-2760

Niskayuna Section
Edwin Reilly, Jr., Supervisor
Town of Niskayuna
One Niskayuna Circle
Niskayuna, NY 12309
(518) 386-4500

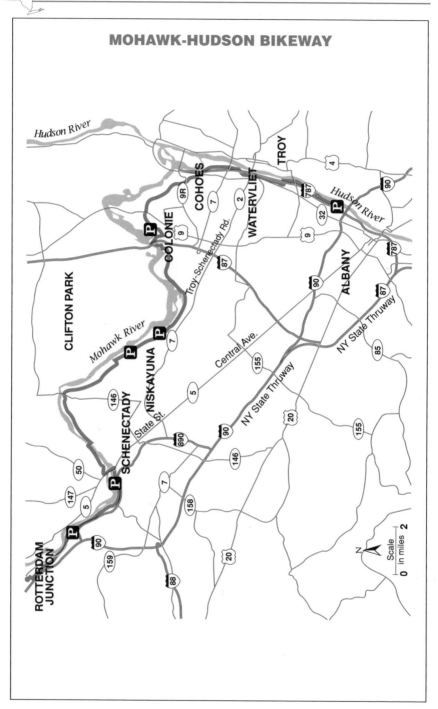

MOHAWK-HUDSON BIKEWAY

Schenectady Section
William Seber, Director
Schenectady Parks and Recreation
City Hall
Jay Street
Schenectady, NY 12305
518-382-5152

Rotterdam Section
Denise Cashmere, Senior Planner
Schenectady County Planning Department
1 Broadway Center
Suite 800
Schenectady, NY 12305
518-386-2225

Pieced together from portions of river valleys, railroad corridors, canals and roadways, the Mohawk-Hudson Bikeway is an urban thoroughfare that should be the envy of any metropolitan area. Originating in the heart of New York's state capital, the trail weaves its way through some of Albany's most populous suburbs before venturing through Schenectady and the pleasant rural countryside beyond. All the while, the trail offers virtually non-stop views of the Mohawk and Hudson Rivers.

Whether you are a commuting cyclist, a recreational runner, an in-line skater or someone who just enjoys the outdoors, you will find something to love about the Mohawk-Hudson Bikeway.

This is not to say that the Mohawk-Hudson is without faults. The piecemeal creation of the trail and its patchwork of management (five people in five different communities are responsible for the trail) lead to inconsistencies. For instance, the trail seems to have a different name everywhere it goes. You will see signs for the Mohawk-Hudson Heritage Trail, the Mohawk River Trailway and the Colonie Bicycle Path among others, although you are unlikely to see a single sign for the Mohawk-Hudson Bikeway.

In addition, mileage markers are placed sporadically along the trail, often starting over from zero each time you cross a town line—although some multi-mile sections have no mileage markers at all. To help resolve confusion, both the Albany and Schenectady County Planning Departments (see addresses and phone numbers above) provide a free, detailed map of the Bikeway. The front features an overview map, and the back shows street-level detail for every section of the trail.

You can begin the trail next to the Hudson River in downtown Albany at the Corning Riverfront Preserve. From northbound Interstate 787, exit at Broadway and stay on the access road until you see the parking area on your right. From southbound I-787, take the exit for Colonie Street and turn left at the end of the ramp. Here you will find an extensive green space dotted with picnic tables and benches, many of which are occupied at lunchtime during warmer months. Rest rooms also are located here. Follow signs for the Corning Fitness Trail. The trail ends 0.3 miles to the right (toward the skyscrapers of Albany) and continues more than 40 miles if you head to the left.

As you travel north, away from downtown, you get glimpses of the Hudson River for the first several miles. You pass a few sculptures and several fitness stations as you head out of the Riverfront Preserve. Remember to turn around and look at the Albany skyline. You pass under Interstate 90 in less than 2 miles, just after you briefly veer away from Interstate 787, which parallels the trail for much of its eastern leg. Some tree roots protrude through the trail surface in this heavily used section, where mileage markers help you log your distance.

Soon after the 4-mile mark, you pass under Route 378, and the interstate reappears on your left. Just past mile 5, you enter a tunnel, cut under I-87 and end up on 4th and Broadway in Watervliet. This town is home to the Watervliet Arsenal, which is used to store and repair firearms. It is the nation's oldest arsenal in continuous use. You travel on-street for about 4 miles, beginning on Broadway, and passing the arsenal in less than a mile. Soon you pass a fast-food restaurant and a small shopping center. In another mile, turn right on Lower Hudson and follow the Bike Route signs. Once you pass Hudson Shores Park, you pick up a bike lane that runs through the town of Green Island.

You can cross the Hudson River on the Troy–Green Island Bridge to take a side trip into downtown Troy, which calls itself

In the town of Colonie, take some time to enjoy the panoramic views of the Mohawk River.

"the home of Uncle Sam." The Troy Riverfront Park is just on the opposite side of the bridge.

To get back to the separated bike path, continue on Lower Hudson (or George) Street, under I-87 and past Paine Street Park, where picnic tables, a playground and rest rooms are available. You turn left onto Tibbets Street, and soon afterward, right onto Cohoes, which turns into Dyke Avenue. After you cautiously cross the four-lane Cohoes Arterial, do not follow Bike Route signs directing you to turn right on Saratoga Street.

Instead, cross Saratoga Street at grade, go over a set of railroad tracks, and up a hill (this is Spring Street, but it is not well marked). Turn left when the street dead ends. After two blocks, turn right on Alexander Street and continue uphill about two blocks to the separated path. You can only take the trail to the right, where a sign reads, "Mohawk River Trailway, Crescent Branch," and another sign tells you that you are 4 miles from Colonie.

This segment of the Bikeway is located on a former Crescent Railroad corridor, and the tree-lined route is a welcome respite from the city streets. And because this rail corridor was built on a ridge, you are now at the same height as most of the rooftops and treetops in the surrounding neighborhood. This section of trail is not as well maintained as other sections; you may see some graffiti on the trail or small pockets of trash. Mileage markers (from 1 to 4) do give you some sense of distance as you travel this short section.

After you pass through a short metal culvert, the views open up to expose a mix of buildings in the town of Cohoes, located at the confluence of the Mohawk and Hudson Rivers. At Vliet Boulevard, you pass through a second culvert, and in a little more than a half-mile, you cross Manor Avenue at-grade. From here, you are about 1.5 miles from Colonie and 12 miles from downtown Albany. This next section, lined with maple and sumac trees, is quite serene.

Soon the trail passes under U.S. Route 9 and wends its way into Colonie Town Park. This park, with a large swimming pool, tennis courts, ball fields, picnic areas, rest rooms and a boat launch, is a pleasant place to stop and relax. Parking is available within the park or in a designated trail parking lot at Schermerhorn Road. Many people begin the trail from here, exploring the western section of trail that parallels the Mohawk River.

The trail's mid-section, from Colonie to Schenectady, is built on a former Troy-Schenectady Railroad corridor. This line opened in 1842, primarily to serve passengers. Penn Central eventually took over the line, and hauled straw, sugar beets and other produce from local farms.

The 5 miles through Colonie are mostly wooded, with a wide variety of trees and wildflowers. Beyond Colonie Town Park, look for dogwood, pin oak, hickory and sugar maple trees. After more than a half-mile, you will be routed on-street to get around Interstate 87. Following signs, turn right on Dunsbach Ferry Road and left on Island View Road. Soon you pass under the I-87 Twin Bridges, which cross the deepest part of the Mohawk River. After a steep incline, you return to the rail corridor just past an out-of-place mileage marker that indicates you have gone a mile from some point in the town of Colonie.

You are now on a ridge, although heavy tree cover obstructs most river views. You actually veer away from the river shortly, as dense woods surround both sides of the trail. After two quick road

Karen-Lee Ryan

This popular trail always attracts a mix of users.

crossings, wetlands begin to line the trail's right side. Woodchucks and foxes inhabit the surrounding area. Beyond mile marker 3, some of the vegetation has been cleared, offering a panoramic view of the river. Take a break on one of the benches that have been strategically placed for optimal viewing.

The next 2 miles are pleasantly wooded and packed with songbirds, as well as a mix of wildflowers, including Queen Anne's lace, black-eyed susans, purple loosestrife and goldenrod. Wetlands continue to line the colorful route as you pass into the town of Niskayuna, where the asphalt looks older and a 0.0 is painted on the pavement.

You soon reach the old Niskayuna Railroad Station with ample parking and rest rooms. You can stop here for a picnic and walk down to the riverbank. This historic railroad structure, which has not yet been refurbished, is near the halfway point of the Mohawk-Hudson Bikeway. New mileage markers begin at the train station for the Niskayuna portion of the trail.

Wetlands resume beyond the station, although they give way to a patch of farmland. Just before Niskayuna's 2-mile mark, a bridge appears to be missing, so you must make a fairly steep

When the trail leaves the railroad grade in the town of Niskayuna, you get some of the best views of the Mohawk River.

descent. At the bottom, you can head right to get to Lock 7 of the Erie Canal, where picnic tables, pay phones and a boat launch are located. A portion of the Mohawk has been "canalized," making the river and the canal one waterway along much of the Mohawk.

Back up on the railroad grade, the corridor remains wooded, with intermittent wetlands and glimpses of the river. Soon you head up a steep hill that veers left (only foot traffic can continue straight), and at the top you reach Blatnick Town Park—another place to take a break. At Niskayuna's 4-mile mark, you pass the Knolls Atomic Power Laboratory, quickly followed by a massive research and development plant for General Electric Company. If it is lunch time, you may see office workers in dress clothes walking along the trail. In this section, the trail has gone off the railroad grade, closely paralleling River Road high above the Mohawk.

Near the 5-mile mark, the trail turns right, before descending a steep hill that ends a mile later with a series of dangerous S curves. You pick up the railroad grade again near the river. The next few miles are flat, straight and wooded, as you travel with ease toward Schenectady. You cross the city limits less than 9 miles from the Niskayuna Railroad Station. The separated trail ends within a mile, dropping you onto Jay Street, the start of a 2-mile on-street jaunt through the "Electric City" of Schenectady. The historic Stockade District (at Jay and State Streets) offers several shops and restaurants. Named for the stockade that surrounded the town in its early days, the Stockade District contains many historic buildings and homes. Take a left on Jay and continue to State Street, where you will find a bicycle-pedestrian thoroughfare.

Schenectady was a one-company town for many years after Thomas Edison moved in and started General Electric Company. While much of the turbine manufacturing business has closed down, the GE Research and Development division (which you passed along the trail) is still located here.

To continue west on the trail, you need to circle underneath State Route 5 (State Street through town). To do this, take State Street toward the river, watching carefully for Schenectady Community College signs. Follow the turn for the college on a road that veers off just before Route 5 crosses the river. You make a large semi-circle, and the separated trail resumes at the bottom. A 0.0 mileage marker is located here, although you are now almost 35 miles from downtown Albany. Parking is available nearby.

For about 4 miles, Interstate 890 lines the left side of the trail. Near the new mile marker 2, watch carefully to the right, and you will see three stone walls that are the remnants of an old canal lock from the original Erie Canal. Soon you may have the opportunity to observe Lock 8 in action. Lock 8 helps boats get around the nearby dam on the Mohawk River. Parking and picnicking are available here, as well as pay phones.

By the 4-mile mark, you are making a slight diversion around interstate ramps. You are now very close to the river and some of the most spectacular river views of your entire journey. Toward the end of this semi-circle—all of which is on a separated trail— you pass through Plotterkill Aqueduct, where you see fields of wildflowers dotted with birdhouses. After passing the aqueduct, you soon approach Kiwanis Park.

The last couple of miles of the Mohawk-Hudson Bikeway follow the original Erie Canal Towpath—a quiet and wooded ending to this 41-mile trail. The Bikeway ends abruptly at a set of active railroad tracks, although you can follow side streets into the small town of Rotterdam Junction. This section of the trail is due to be extended another 1.5 miles toward the town of Pattersonville during the summer of 1996.

7. North County Trailway

Endpoints: Eastview to Hawthorne and Hawthorne to Kitchawan

Location: Westchester County

Length: 12.5 miles (will be 22 miles when completed)

Surface: Asphalt

Uses:

Contact: David DeLucia, Director of Park Facilities
Westchester County Parks and Recreation
19 Bradhurst Avenue
Hawthorne, NY 10532
914-593-2600

◆◆◆

In a region dependent on commuter trains, it is fitting that the North County Trailway is constructed on a rail line that served commuters for more than 75 years. Located in the shadows of New York City, this Westchester County rail-trail is easily accessible from an interstate highway and two parkways.

Constructed primarily on the Putnam Division of the New York Central Railroad, the North County Trailway has replaced what from 1881 to 1958 commuters referred to as the "Old Put." Once serving 23 stations in Westchester County, the Putnam line carried passengers from the Bronx in New York City to Brewster in Putnam County, traversing Westchester County on the way. Today, 12.5 miles of this corridor have been converted into the North County Trailway.

This trail is still a work in progress, and you may want to check with the trail manager to get the latest information on what is open and accessible. In the summer of 1995, two sections of the

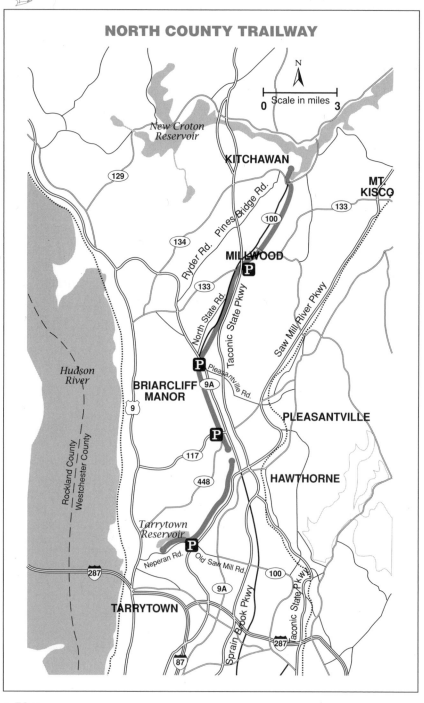

NORTH COUNTY TRAILWAY

N

Scale in miles
0   3

New Croton Reservoir

KITCHAWAN

MT. KISCO

129

133

100

134

Ryder Rd.   Pines Bridge Rd.

MILLWOOD

133

North State Rd.

Taconic State Pkwy

Saw Mill River Pkwy

Hudson River

9A

Pleasantville Rd.

BRIARCLIFF MANOR

9

PLEASANTVILLE

117

448

HAWTHORNE

Rockland County
Westchester County

Tarrytown Reservoir

Neperan Rd.   Old Saw Mill Rd.

100

287

9A

Taconic State Pkwy

TARRYTOWN

Sprain Brook Pkwy

287

87

trail were currently open, with only about 500 yards in Hawthorne separating them. Unfortunately, this short distance was completely impassable, although it is slated to open by spring 1997 as the Taconic Parkway and other nearby state routes are reconstructed. Currently, the southern section is just less than 3 miles long and the northern section is about 9.5 miles long. In 1995, a third, 5-mile segment in the north was under construction from Yorktown Heights to the Putnam County line. The two short gaps that will connect these three sections into a 22-mile trail are slated to open in 1997. Ultimately, the county plans to develop a continuous 36.2-mile trail from the Putnam County line all the way south to the border of the Bronx. When this happens, the North County Trailway will connect with the Old Putnam Trail in the Bronx (see page 77).

Eastview to Hawthorne

To get to the southern section of the North County Trailway, take Interstate 87 north from New York City to Exit 7A, the Saw Mill River Parkway and continue north on the Parkway to Exit 23/ Eastview. (If you prefer, you can also take the Parkway north from New York City all the way to the Eastview Exit.) As you exit, turn west (left) onto Old Saw Mill River Road. After crossing under the Parkway, you pass the start of the trail on the right side of the road. Continue a short distance farther and park in the free Park & Ride lot, also on the right side of the road.

From the Park & Ride lot, you can get onto the North County Trailway, or you can cross Old Saw Mill River Road to take a short 1-mile jaunt along the Tarrytown Reservoir, which looks like a large pond. This quiet, tree-lined route is a pleasant, informal extension of the southern section of the North County Trail, which parallels the Saw Mill River Parkway for its 2.7 mile distance.

Once on the North County Trailway, you can hear and often see the traffic on the Parkway, although the corridor itself is nestled amid a canopy of trees. The trail is quite flat, and generally raised above the level of the Parkway. About 2 miles from the parking area, you cross under some power lines. You pass the headquarters for the County Police before the trail ends near the junction of the Saw Mill River Parkway, the Taconic Parkway and State Route 9A. At this point it is not possible to connect to the northern section, although this gap in the trail is slated for construction in 1997.

Hawthorne to Kitchawan

Although the trail continues only 500 yards from where the first segment ends, you cannot access the trail in this area. The best place to get onto the trail is in Mount Pleasant, where a parking lot is located to service the trail. To reach it, take the Saw Mill River Parkway north to the Taconic Parkway and exit at State Route 117 and head west. As soon as you pass the junction of Routes 9A and 100, you can see the trail continuing on the right side under high tension power lines. A parking lot is located directly across from the trail on the left side of Route 117.

You can travel south, back toward the gap, along the highway for 2 miles. The setting is pleasant and similar to the first section of trail. If you travel north, Routes 9A and 100 line your right side, although a thin band of trees keeps the setting green. Hardwood trees also dot the left side, where power lines tower above on a hill. Similar to the trail's southern segment, this section of trail remains elevated from the busy highway.

As you approach the 1-mile mark you cross the Pocantico River on a short wooden bridge. You pass by a few homes on the left before the trail briefly cuts between 9A and an entrance ramp. By the time you have traveled 1.5 miles, the power lines have veered away from the trail and soon some rocky outcroppings line your left side. You pass under Pleasantville Road before traversing the edge of Law Memorial Park. If you venture off the trail into the park, you will find various amenities, including soccer fields, tennis courts, a swimming pool, rest rooms and parking. In the vicinity, you can also find the Briarcliff Public Library, housed in one of the original railroad stations of the "Old Put."

As you near the 2-mile mark, Route 9A splits off from Route 100. You continue to parallel Route 100, traveling on the shoulder for about a half-mile. Near the town of Briarcliff Manor, the trail resumes as a separated path. This mile-long section of trail initially parallels the Pocantico River and is shielded from the road by thick vegetation. In less than a half-mile, you cross lightly-traveled Old Chappaqua Road.

When the separated trail ends in another half-mile, you are technically on the right shoulder of Route 100, although you may

Westchester County Department of Parks, Recreation & Conservation

While the North County Trailway runs through an urban setting, it also features plenty of tranquil spots along the way.

feel sandwiched between this highway and the Taconic Parkway, which now lines your right side. A guard rail separates you from both roads, and the trail remains surprisingly pleasant with a mix of maple, locust and willow trees in the vicinity.

Within a half-mile (about 4 miles from the parking lot) the guard rail ends, placing you truly on the shoulder of Route 100. By now, the Taconic Parkway has veered away. After passing a sizable outcropping of rocks on your right side, you reach Echo Lake, also on the right. Late in the day, the trees encircling the lake reflect colorfully in the placid water. Beyond the lake, you pass under the Taconic Parkway before the trail resumes as a separate path—and remains that way until it ends in Kitchawan.

As the separated trail begins, you parallel Station Road, which features a grocery store, a drug store, a restaurant and a post office—the first accessible services in several miles. You pass a former railroad station, now painted red and white, before crossing Millwood Road as you enter the town of New Castle.

After you pass under some power lines, the trail becomes progressively more wooded. Beyond West Orchard Road, where limited parking is available, residences line much of the trail's left side. About 1.5 miles from Millwood Road (nearly 6 miles from your starting point) the trail crosses over State Route 100 on an attractive steel trestle. You are heading noticeably downhill as you cut under Route 134 via a metal culvert about 0.3 miles later.

You are now on the southern end of the 208-acre Kitchawan County Park Preserve. A historical sign with information about the former railroad corridor is located on the trail's left side soon before the trail ends abruptly 0.2 miles beyond Route 134. A huge body of water known as the New Croton Reservoir lies just north of here, where a massive, multi-trestled railroad bridge spans the reservoir. Until this is developed, you will not be able to continue any farther north on this segment of trail.

This bridge—and the remainder of the undeveloped corridor—will eventually connect with the new northern section between Yorktown Heights and the Putnam County Line. When this happens, Westchester County will have a continuous 22-mile trail. Plans also call for acquiring and developing a 14-mile southern segment between Eastview and the Old Putnam Trail in the Bronx.

8. Old Erie Canal State Park

Endpoints: DeWitt to Rome

Location: Madison, Oneida and Onondaga Counties

Length: 35.5 miles

Surface: Crushed stone

Uses:

🚴 ♿ on certain sections

Contact: Kenneth Showalter, Park Manager
Old Erie Canal State Park
New York State Office of Parks, Recreation
  and Historic Preservation
Andrus Road
Kirkville, NY 13082
315-687-7821

◆◆◆

Beginning about 8 miles from downtown Syracuse, the Old Erie Canal State Park cuts through magnificent central New York countryside. The trail was created on the towpath of the original 363-mile Erie Canal and currently serves as a showpiece for a statewide trail system based on canals. Proximity to two sizable state parks makes the Old Erie Canal State Park a place to visit again and again.

Construction of the original Erie Canal began in the tiny town of Rome on July 4, 1817. The first phase of the canal connected the cities of Utica and Syracuse. It was known as The Great Level because the route had few obstructions and required no lift locks. When the 363-mile canal was opened across the state in 1825,

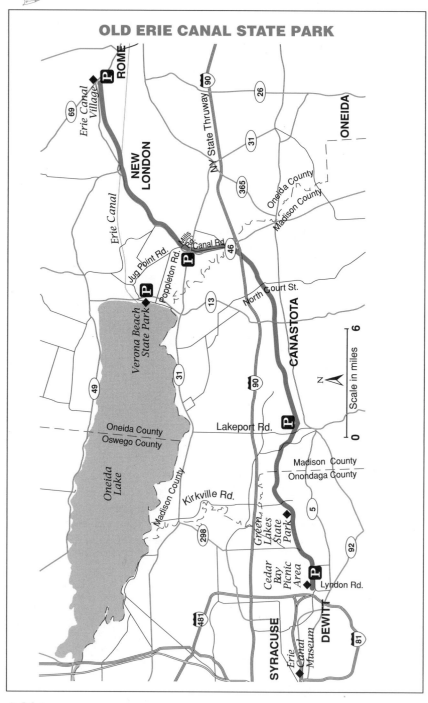

OLD ERIE CANAL STATE PARK

it was considered the foremost engineering achievement of its time. Additional canals—including the Oswego, Champlain and Cayuga-Seneca Canals—soon opened, earning New York its reputation as a state that could build empires.

While many of these original canals surrendered to other forms of transportation, New York is fueling new life into them today by creating the 524-mile Statewide Canalway Trail System. This progressive recreation plan will preserve a key part of New York's industrial heritage, while protecting valuable open space and providing an array of recreational activities to millions of residents and visitors.

To get to the Old Erie Canal State Park, take State Route 5/92 east from Interstate 481. In 1.2 miles, the two routes split. At this point, turn left onto Lyndon Road. Proceed 1 mile to the Cedar Bay Picnic Area, which is the trail's eastern parking lot.

This picnic area, which offers many tables, grills, a swing set and rest rooms, is a pleasant start to a beautifully developed trail. To get down to the canal towpath, go past the rest rooms and cross over the canal on a small footbridge; the trail begins at the bottom of the incline. If you go left, the trail ends anticlimactically in less than a mile. If you go right, you will pass the 1-mile mark almost immediately, and you can continue on the trail for another 34.5 miles all the way to Rome.

Intermittent bands of trees—including sugar and red maple, sumac and weeping willow—hug the route for the first couple of miles, while rolling mountains can be seen in the distance. At the 1.6-mile mark, you make your first at-grade crossing at Burdick Street, and you will see some of the trail's superior signing features. They indicate what road you are crossing and how far it is to the next landmark.

The next few miles feel quite rural, although you are still less than 10 miles outside of Syracuse. Gently rolling terrain lines the left side, while the canal and Route 290 run along your right. You pass through Green Lakes State Park at the trail's 4.6-mile mark. You may want to spend some time in this 1,700-acre park, which offers a host of diversions. You can even rent a cabin or camp to make full use of the park's facilities, including a sandy beach with a concession stand, boat rentals, an 18-hole golf course, picnic tables, ball fields and a series of trails for hiking and

Karen-Lee Ryan

The Old Erie Canal State Park begins just a few miles east of Syracuse.

snowshoeing. You also will find rest rooms here, as well as plenty of parking.

The trail continues along its pleasant, wooded way for several more miles, and you might catch a glimpse of a woodchuck, a beaver, a raccoon or a white-tailed deer—all of which are plentiful in this area.

About 1.5 miles from the park, you skirt the small town of Kirkville. Soon thereafter, you cross Poolsbrook Road at grade, which is followed by a grassy picnic area with many shade trees. A footbridge before the 8-mile mark will take you to a picnic area, where more parking is available. Another place to stop is the Chittenango Landing Canal Boat Museum located about 3 miles farther east.

You can access the museum, which is open a few days a week in summer and limited times during the fall, by taking a right at Lakeport Road, just prior to the 11-mile mark. Even if the museum is closed, you should venture to the other side of the canal to see this site, which is still under development. In 1855, a canal boat building and repair service were established here, as well as three dry docks and a sawmill-blacksmith complex. The entire area shut down in 1917; the dry docks were filled and buildings demolished. A historic preservation project currently is helping to replicate these structures. This project is completely volunteer driven. When completed, the area will feature extensive historical interpretation of canal boats and the people associated with the canal. For information on the Canal Boat Museum, call 315-687-3801.

If you need food or supplies before continuing on the trail, you can proceed south on Lakeport Road about a half-mile into Chittenango, where you will find several fast food restaurants and gas stations. The next few miles of trail are fairly open, offering nice views of the rolling countryside that surrounds you. Within 5 miles, you will be heading into the town of Canastota, where the trail goes on-road for about a half-mile, beginning at State Street, which is located near the 16.5 mile mark.

As you travel out of town, you begin paralleling Canal Road and a few industrial areas. After about 2 miles, you reach North Court Street (at the 19.5-mile mark), where you need to make a one-block detour off the trail. The canal goes under busy Court Street, but the trail jogs around it. Soon Canal Road resumes on your left, with fields and woods beyond. Meanwhile, on the right, the canal continues to parallel the trail. The surface in this section is a bit chunkier than earlier sections.

When you reach Cobb Street, you are near the New York State Thruway. The trail briefly goes on-street to cross the highway, although it immediately resumes as a separate trail on the other side of the bridge. You continue paralleling Canal Road until you reach State Route 316 near the town of Durhamville. After this at-grade crossing, the trail abruptly stops at State Route 46.

A 2.2-mile section of trail has not yet been developed in this area. To get around this section, you have two options: go north on busy Route 46 or on the lightly traveled Canal Road. To get to Canal Road, diagonally cross Route 46 to get onto Center Street, and then make an immediate left onto Oneida Street. You cross over the canal and pass by the Durhamville Fire Department before turning right onto Canal Road, a pleasant residential street.

More than a mile into this detour, you see an intriguing small footbridge on your left. Canal Road ends at State Route 31.

To get back to the trail, take a left and an immediate right (to get across the canal), and the trail resumes on the right. Route 46 parallels the trail on the left for the next several miles, while the canal continues on the right.

A small parking area with interpretive signs has been built at the trail's 25-mile mark. From here, you can take a side trip to Verona Beach State Park, located on spectacular Oneida Lake just a few miles northwest of this point. To get there, take a left on Mills Road and jog across to Jug Point Road. In less than a mile, this road veers left and turns into Poppleton Road, which leads to the state park in 2.5 miles.

This 1,735-acre park offers an entire day's worth of activities: swimming along an expansive, ocean-like beach; picnicking at tables or in shelters; and riding horseback or hiking on several park trails. In the winter, this is a popular spot for cross-country skiing, ice fishing and snowmobiling. The park also offers rest rooms, parking, a seasonal concession stand and camping in a wooded setting.

Back on the canal, the trail switches to the right side of the canal, offering a welcome separation from Route 46, which lines

Many historic buildings line the trail, including this one near DeWitt.

the canal's left side. The next few miles are significantly more remote than previous sections of the canal, with only an occasional barn dotting the landscape. Higginsville Road seems to be the only sign that you are passing through a town called Higginsville at mile marker 27.

In 2.3 miles, you reach Lock Road, where you go on-street for a half-mile. You cross over a bridge and take an immediate right to reach Lock 21 of the existing Erie Canal. The trail traverses this modern-day canal for a short distance before resuming along the original canal in New London. At this point, you are less than 5 miles from the Erie Canal Village in Rome.

After crossing Zingerline Road, wetlands surround the canal, and the setting becomes even more remote. Maples, American beech, aspen and an occasional white pine line the route until Fort Bull Road at the 35-mile mark. At this point the views open up, and you can see the Erie Canal Village ahead of you. A footbridge across the canal signals your entrance into this attraction, which is run by the city of Rome.

The Erie Canal Village commemorates the site where the Erie Canal began, and it is a fun place to end your trip on the Old Erie Canal State Park. In addition to viewing the historic exhibits here, you can also take canal boat rides and get something to eat. To get information on hours of operation or admission prices, call the Erie Canal Village at 315-337-3999.

Karen-Lee Ryan

Portions of the old Erie Canal have been refilled with water.

9. Old Erie Canal Towpath Trail

Endpoints: Camillus to Port Byron

Location: Onondaga and Cayuga Counties

Length: 20 miles

Surface: Gravel and dirt

Uses: 🚶 🚴 🐎 ⛷ 🛶

Contact: Dr. David Beebe, Director
Town of Camillus Erie Canal Park
5750 Devoe Road
Camillus, NY 13031
315-488-3409 or 315-672-5110

◆◆◆

If you are interested in combining some history with a rugged recreational experience, you may want to plan a trip to the Old Erie Canal Towpath Trail. For more than two decades a small corps of volunteers has been working to restore the Camillus to Port Byron section of the old Erie Canal to its former state—complete with bridges, locks, buildings and a towpath. You can visit some of these developed facilities in the town of Camillus and continue on the canal's towpath for nearly 20 miles.

This section of the canal was built in the mid-1800s during the enlargement of the Erie Canal. The enlargement included the Nine Mile Creek Aqueduct, which was built in Camillus in 1844 and today is listed on the National Register of Historic Places. The development of the New York State Barge Canal System forced the abandonment of this enlarged segment in 1922. Camillus Township purchased seven miles of the canal in 1972. At that time, volunteers began to restore the canal to its original

OLD ERIE CANAL TOWPATH TRAIL

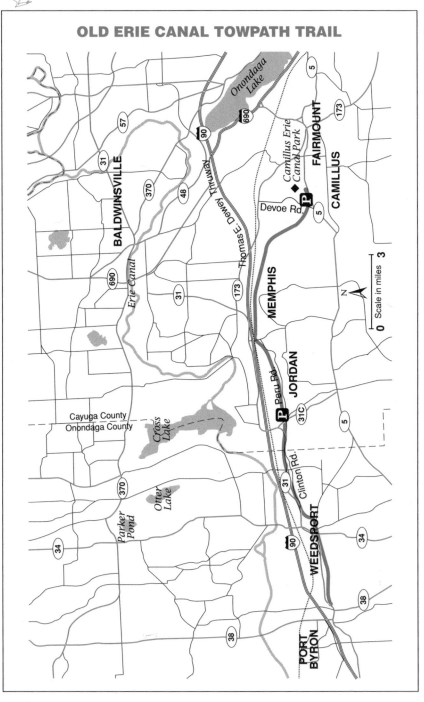

splendor, filling it with water and repairing the towpath by clearing brush and building bridges.

While the effort is still a work in progress, the highlight of the volunteers' efforts can be found in the Town of Camillus Erie Canal Park. Here, volunteers have built a replica of Sims Store, which was one of many stores that sold supplies to canal workers and travelers. The original Sims Store was destroyed by fire in 1963, and the newly built replica serves as the park's headquarters. If you visit the store, you will see that the first floor is set up to look like the original store. The second floor serves as a museum with early photos and maps of the canal, models of locks and aqueducts and other exhibits. Outside, volunteers offer canal boat rides on Sundays May through October.

Camillus Landing, located near the town park, was the mid-point of the Enlarged Erie Canal that spanned the state. A sign across from Sims Store shows two arrows pointing in opposite directions with the accompanying text: 175 miles to Albany; 177 miles to Buffalo.

Located just a few miles west of Syracuse, the Town of Camillus Erie Canal Park is the best place to absorb some history of the Erie Canal and begin your trail excursion. To get there, take State Route 5 west out of Syracuse. In the town of Camillus, turn north (right) onto Newport Road. In a block turn right again onto Devoe Road, where a sign directs you to the park.

After you've explored the park—and maybe even taken a short boat ride on the canal to view the Nine Mile Creek Aqueduct—you may want to head west on the canal towpath. To the east, the canal and towpath end in 2 miles. A towpath trail exists on both sides of the canal only in the vicinity of this park, so if you plan to go any distance on the trail, stay on the side of the canal where Sims Store is located. Also, be aware that the eastern end of this trail is significantly more developed than the majority of the route, which is more suitable for mountain biking, hiking and horseback riding.

As you head west, the towpath is quite wide and road-like for the first several miles. After crossing Devoe Road, you skirt the edge of a wildlife refuge. You arrive at Warner's Community Park in 2 miles. Here, you find swing sets, picnic tables, grills and a pavilion, all surrounded by a pleasant grassy setting.

The next mile of trail doubles as a road. The road ends at a mound of dirt, and trail users can continue on the other side of it. As you proceed west, the towpath becomes a bit more rugged, as it has not yet been developed and is only lightly used. The trail gradually becomes an overgrown single-track corridor, and the quiet wooded setting remains pleasant.

As you pass through the tiny hamlet of Memphis near the 5-mile mark, the trail is practically a rail-with-trail, with active Conrail tracks closely paralleling the canal towpath. In another mile you reach Laird Road, where you may see "No Trespassing signs." To get around this detour, jog right and immediately left onto Powerhouse Road. In less than a mile, the road veers sharply left and becomes McDonald Road; follow this for about a half-mile. The canal and towpath resume on the right.

Once back on the towpath, you immediately see some stone walls on the right side, which are remnants of an old lock. An area known as McGraw Swamp lines the trail's right side for more than a half-mile, before you begin cutting through a small residential area. The canal is wide (although generally dry) in this area, where some homeowners use the towpath as an access road.

Volunteers operate canal boat rides in Camillus.

Karen-Lee Ryan

You can view the canal's beautiful stonework in the town of Jordan.

About 9 miles from the Town of Camillus Erie Canal Park, you enter the town of Jordan and a small community park, located next to a housing development called Old Erie Place. The park offers a few picnic tables and grills, as well as parking for about a dozen cars. You need to travel on-street through Jordan for about 0.3 miles, passing in front of the area high school. Just beyond the high school, you can see the route of the canal, which now serves as a grassy open space in town.

You will see original stonework off to your left before crossing a short bridge and proceeding on the wide canal-turned-greenway through Jordan. If you have some time, take a side trip through town via Jordan Road to get a glimpse of some well-preserved Colonial-style architecture—virtually every house has columns. Back on the trail, you pass behind a steepled church and several homes before reaching heavily-traveled Route 31, which you will cross at grade. At this point, you are about 5 miles away from Weedsport, the next town on the trail with any services.

For the next couple of miles, you closely parallel Route 31. The trail is densely wooded and again quite narrow until you cross into Cayuga County about 1.5 miles from Jordan. The next mile of trail was under development in 1995, when a crushed stone surface was put down on a short section of trail.

After the stretch of new trail, you cross Route 31 at grade, returning to a narrow, densely-wooded corridor for a mile before crossing back over Route 31. At this point, you may want to take Canal Road (on your right) for about a mile. Shortly after the road curves left, you can resume the trail on your right side.

When you approach the intersection of Routes 31 and 34, the trail seems to end in the parking lot of a fast food restaurant. The towpath and trail are not continuous through the town of Weedsport. If you want to continue another 4 miles into Port Byron get onto Route 31, which is Main Street through town. You pass the Museum of History on your way, which offers a pleasant diversion from the trail. On the western edge of town, turn right on Watson Street to pick up the canal and towpath again on your left.

The corridor remains wooded until you reach the trail's current terminus in Port Byron. You may want to venture through this historic town, where a canal-era hotel is located and a canal museum is under construction.

10. Old Putnam Trail

Endpoints: Van Cortlandt Park in the Bronx,
New York City

Location: Bronx County

Length: 1.25 miles

Surface: Wood chips and dirt

Uses:

Contact: Marianne Anderson
Special Projects Coordinator
Van Cortlandt and Pelham Bay Parks
   Administration
1 Bronx River Parkway
Bronx, NY 10462
718-430-1890

◆◆◆

When you think of the Bronx, wildflowers, wetlands, and wildlife are not what usually spring to mind. But, if you take a walk on the Old Putnam Trail, it's extactly what you'll find. Visitors to this oasis in the big city will want to travel this trail slowly to truly absorb the diversity of the plant and animal life.

Thousands of years ago, this area was a popular hunting and fishing spot for native Americans, who also farmed this land for a few hundred years before the first European settlers arrived in the mid-1600s. The park was established in 1888 to honor the Van Cortlandt family. This prestigious family produced two New York City mayors, the first of whom (Augustus Van Cortlandt) is famous for hiding the city's records in the family's burial vault—now located in Van Cortlandt Park—to keep this information out of the hands of the British during the Revolutionary War.

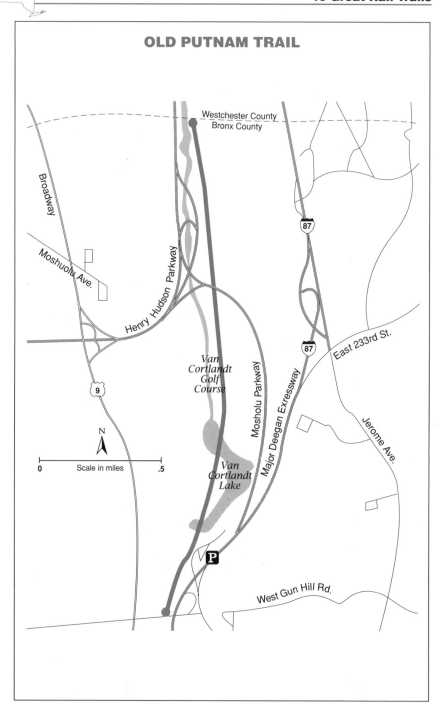

OLD PUTNAM TRAIL

Karen-Lee Ryan

The Parade Ground in Van Cortlandt Park lines the trail's west side.

Two railroad tracks operated through the park. The longer surviving line was operated by the Putnam Division of the New York Central Railroad. Known as the "Old Put," it ran from the High Bridge in the Bronx to Brewster in Putnam County, carrying passengers and freight between 1881 and 1958. Occasional freight service continued on the line until 1981. This is the same line that has been converted into the North County Trailway in Westchester County (see page 57), and one day the two trails will meet.

To get to Van Cortlandt Park and the Old Putnam Trail, take the Van Cortlandt South Exit from Interstate 87 (Major Deegan Expressway) and follow the signs for the Van Cortlandt Golf Course. It will seem like you are about to get back onto I-87, but the road to the golf course forks away from the highway ramp and leads into a sizable parking lot. You can get onto the trail to the left of the golf house, at the southwest corner of Van Cortlandt Lake. Incidentally, the popular golf course that surrounds much of the trail is America's oldest public golf course.

As you make your way from the parking lot onto the trail, use the double-track railroad bridge to cross the lake. If you head to the left, you will soon reach the remnants of the Old Van Cortlandt

Railroad Station. Beyond this point, the trail gets progressively more overgrown as you approach the park's boundary. Your best bet after exploring this end of the trail is to retrace the short distance you have traveled so that you can continue more than a mile to the north.

Heading north, the trail doubles as the John Kieran Nature Trail for the first 0.3 miles. This trail is a 1-mile loop that you also may want to explore. A large open area known as the Parade Ground lines your left side, although a fence temporarily separates you from it. There are breaks in the fence with steps made of railroad ties leading into the park. (You will have several opportunities to access the Parade Ground along the way.) The right side is fairly densely wooded with Van Cortlandt Lake beyond.

Within 0.2 miles, the corridor opens up offering a view of a surprisingly large wetland to your left. You cross the lake on another railroad bridge and the wetland continues. This is a freshwater marsh, and it is bursting with buttonbush, cattails and reeds. In addition, a mix of birds and wildlife flock to the area. It may be hard to imagine spotting a great blue heron, an egret, a red-winged blackbird or a pair of wood ducks in the Bronx, but if you observe this marsh quietly—even for a short time—you are bound to see at least one. You may also see several aquatic insects, including waterstriders and dragonflies.

Soon the John Kieran Nature Trail veers off to the left, arcing west past a small pool that is home to many bullfrogs, before turning south through the Parade Ground and leading back to the parking lot. You may want to take this route on your return trip to get a different perspective on the area.

Continuing north on the Old Putnam Trail, wetlands yield to views of the golf course, which now surrounds the trail beyond its lightly wooded perimeter. Railroad tracks are often underfoot, which help keep you to a slow pace. If you take some time to look around, you will be amazed at the wide variety of trees in this urban setting. They include a mix of hickory, sassafras, tulip, mulberry and a number of maples.

Beyond the half-mile mark, you pass under Mosholu Parkway, where you are (unfortunately) bound to see some graffiti and trash. The trail is not maintained as well beyond the overpass, and vegetation creeps into the corridor. As you near the 1-mile mark,

Stone Pillars

Karen-Lee Ryan

These intriguing stone structures still stand along the Old Putnam Trail.

Heading north on the Old Putnam Trail, you are likely to see a series mysterious stone pillars on your left several hundred yards from the parking lot. While littered with graffiti, these structures still hold an interesting tale.

Erected around the turn of the century, these 13 pillars were made of stone from various quarries in the Northeast and Midwest. The New York Central Railroad placed them here to test each stone's durability and color for possible use on the facade of the "new" Grand Central Station in Manhattan.

In the end, the railroad selected an Indiana Limestone (actually imported from Illinois) because it could be inexpensively transported on the New York Central's own tracks. The two pillars at the south end of the series are made of Indiana Limestone.

you pass a stone marker, indicating that you are 6 miles from where the train originated at High Bridge.

The golf course soon ends, and if you are so inclined, you can continue about a quarter-mile to the trail's current terminus at the Saw Mill River Parkway. This section of trail is more overgrown, in part because it is less frequently used. One day, this rail-trail will stretch more than 36 miles from the Bronx across Westchester County all the way to Brewster in Putnam County.

11. Oswego County Recreation Trail

Endpoints: Cleveland to Fulton

Location: Oswego County

Length: 28 miles

Surface: Original ballast, made primarily of cinder and dirt

Uses: 🚶 🚴 🐴 ⛷ 🛶

Contact: Brian Madigan, Planner
Oswego County Planning Office
46 East Bridge Street
Oswego, NY 13126-2123
315-349-8292

◆◆◆

In many ways, the Oswego County Recreation Trail seems to begin and end in the middle of nowhere, which is perfect if you are looking to get away from it all.

Actually, the trail begins in a small town on the shores of Oneida Lake and travels through rural—and extremely flat—central New York (passing only one town and several enclaves) on its way to the outskirts of a former railroad hub. And, the trail is part of a much larger snowmobiling network, so if you are a warm-weather trail user, you may be among only a handful of people on the trail. Originally run by the Ontario and Western Railroad, the route has been maintained as a multi-use recreational trail since the late 1970s.

The eastern end of the trail is located in the tiny town of Cleveland, just a few blocks north of Oneida Lake. From the Syracuse area, take Interstate 81 north to State Route 49 east and travel

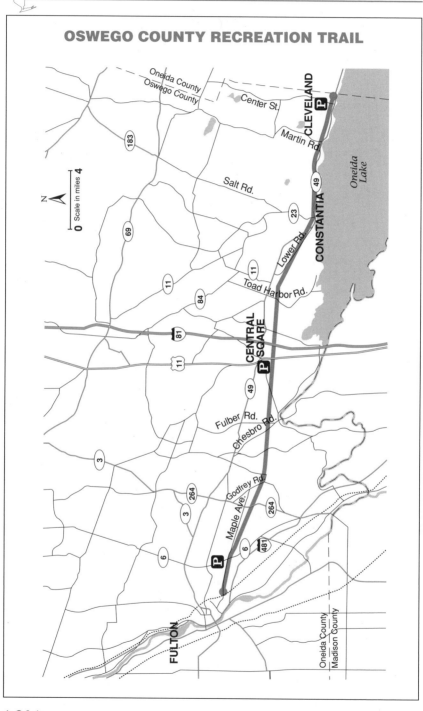

OSWEGO COUNTY RECREATION TRAIL

nearly 15 miles into the town of Cleveland. Turn left onto Center Street, and you will cross the trail corridor in about 0.3 miles. There is parking available on Sand Street (a right turn off of Center Street) near an abandoned glass works factory. The trail is generally considered local, so few parking areas have been developed. The County plans to seek funding for the development of trailhead parking lots in the future.

For management purposes, the trail ends at the Oswego County line, just east of Cleveland. However, the corridor does continue—although it gets progressively narrower—for about 4 miles to the east. If you do opt to travel these miles, be prepared for thick vegetation and wet conditions.

Beginning the trail from Center Street and heading west, you will immediately notice that the trail is quite wide, not to mention straight as a yardstick. The trail's perimeter is lined with a mix of hardwoods and an occasional coniferous tree. You make your first at-grade road crossing in a half-mile. For the next few miles, the corridor passes through some sparsely developed residential areas.

About 2 miles from Cleveland, you make a few road crossings in the town of Bernhards Bay. If you take a left on any of them, you head directly to the scenic shores of Oneida Lake, less than a half-mile away. Near the 4.5-mile mark, the band of trees surrounding the trail thins out, opening up views of the surrounding rural landscape. In another mile, you enter the town of Constantia, another lakefront community. If you have not yet taken a detour to Oneida Lake, this town is one of the last chances to do so, as the trail soon begins heading north.

You pass a small county office building nearly 6 miles from Cleveland, as power lines tower overhead. Soon you cross Route 49 at grade, so use caution. For the next 2 miles, you parallel Lower Road, although you may not notice it. The area surrounding this section of trail is only lightly populated, with an occasional house dotting the otherwise open landscape. Off to the left is Three Mile Bay Wildlife Management Area, and to the right, Toad Harbor Swamp.

You cross Depot Drive and pass a few parking spaces in the hamlet of West Munro near the 9-mile mark. In less than a mile, you cross Toad Harbor Road, and you will know you are in the

The only sign to indicate your location is placed at a road crossing near Fulton.

middle of a preserved open space. There are virtually no trees to obstruct the trail's most scenic vistas, and thousands of cattails are an obvious sign that the surrounding area is a wetland.

In about 2 miles, you reach State Route 37, where you need to travel on-road to detour around Interstate 81 and an active Conrail line. Oswego County has applied for federal funding to build a trail crossing over I-81 and to improve other aspects of the trail. In the meantime, turn right onto Route 37 and left onto Route 49. Head west on Route 49 for 2 miles and then turn south onto U.S. Route 11, the main thoroughfare in the town of Central Square. After 0.6 miles, turn right into the Village Pharmacy shopping plaza before the Ford dealership. The trail resumes at the southern end of the parking lot on the right side. (If you look left, you can see a depot and barricades preventing access to the trail near the active railroad tracks.)

Central Square is the trail's midway point, and several restaurants and gas stations can be found here. In addition, the Central Square Railroad Museum might be worth a short detour, call (315) 676-7582 for hours and information. The remainder of the trail is quite rural, so if you need anything before you get to Fulton, try to find it here.

Continuing west from Central Square, the trail almost immediately passes behind a high school before easing into rural countryside that dominates the trail's surroundings all the way to Fulton. About 3.5 miles from Central Square, you cross State Route 33, where you pass by a feed company on your left. A ribbon of trees continues to line each side of the trail, and in another mile, you cross Route 10.

Before the 20-mile mark, you reach Route 54, where you will see a sign that says "Bridge Closed Ahead." (This is one of the other projects for which the county is hoping to receive funding.) The short bridge over Fish Creek is not decked for trail use, so you need to take a left onto Route 54. Then go one block and turn right. If you look to the right you will see the railroad bridge, and if you are paying attention, you will also see an intriguing stone marker on the road that indicates you are 306 miles from New York City. At the stop sign, veer right and resume the trail on your left.

The trail remains flat and straight while the surroundings feel increasingly remote for another 4 miles. At this point, a short distance from Fulton, you actually pass under a banner-type sign that reads, "Oswego County Recreation Trail." You immediately cross busy Route 6 at grade, so use caution. (If you are interested starting your trail trip from Fulton, some trail parking is available on Route 6.)

You begin to closely parallel Maple Avenue, and the trail ends anticlimactically when it intersects with Maple in 1.5 miles. To get into the town of Fulton (where you will find a few fast food restaurants amid a fairly industrial downtown) turn left on Maple Avenue. Cross two sets of railroad tracks and veer right where Maple comes to a T intersection. In another mile, turn left on Fay Street and follow it into downtown.

In addition to places to eat, Fulton also has developed a scenic riverwalk along the Oswego Canalway. This canal is part of the greater New York State Barge Canal that still enables boats to travel from Lake Ontario all the way to New York City.

Leona K. Jensen

Take time to explore the remains of former industrial buildings along the Outlet Trail.

12. Outlet Trail

Endpoints: Dresden to Penn Yan

Location: Yates County

Length: 7.5 miles

Surface: Asphalt and original ballast

Uses:

on certain sections

Contact: Virginia Gibbs, County Historian
Yates County
110 Court Street, Room 3
Penn Yan, NY 14527-1130
315-536-5147

◆◆◆

Taking a trip on the Outlet Trail is like taking a trip back in time—if you know what to look for. The trail parallels a river-like body of water known as the Keuka Lake Outlet, which formed nearly 10,000 years ago to connect the Keuka and Seneca Finger Lakes. Of course, that's a recent development compared to the three distinctive layers of rock you'll see along your journey—all of which were created some 350 million years ago.

And, if you are interested in America's industrial heritage, seeing the remnants of the dozens of mills that thrived along the Outlet during the 1800s and early 1900s will fascinate you. In fact, this area is so steeped in history that the trail and mill sites have recently been added to the New York State Register of Historic Places.

While native Americans probably fished heavily along the Outlet, the area was used only as a thoroughfare until the first

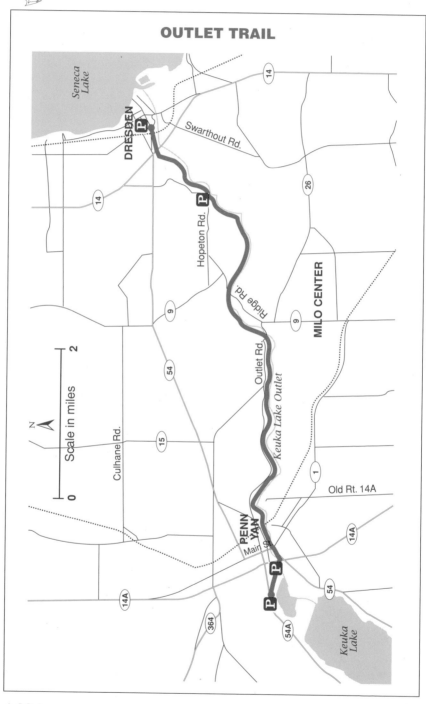

OUTLET TRAIL

Seneca Lake

DRESDEN

Swarthout Rd.

Hopeton Rd.

Ridge Rd.

Outlet Rd.

Keuka Lake Outlet

MILO CENTER

N

Scale in miles

Culhane Rd.

PENN YAN

Main St.

Old Rt. 14A

Keuka Lake

European settlers arrived in 1788. The area now known as Dresden quickly grew to be the largest settlement in western New York because the Outlet provided the hydropower needed to fuel mills. By 1827, a dozen dams had been constructed between Dresden and Penn Yan. Each dam served two or more mills, including gristmills, sawmills, linseed oil mills, tanneries, plaster mills and distilleries.

The Crooked Lake Canal, which runs parallel to the Outlet on the north side, was built to help move farm products to eastern markets. Developed on the heels of the successful Erie Canal, the Crooked Lake Canal opened for business in 1833. Unfortunately, because of its excruciatingly slow pace and 28 lift locks, the canal was in business only 44 years, losing money every year of its operation.

The Penn Yan & New York Railroad opened a line along the former canal towpath in 1884, quickly replacing the obsolete canal in that served the farms and mills along the Outlet. Economic misfortune began striking the region around the turn of the century, and by the time of the Depression many mills had been abandoned or burned in a series of fires that racked the region. The last mill shut down before 1950, and the corridor was finally abandoned in 1972 after it was damaged by a flood. The county purchased the corridor in 1981.

Today you can trace much of this history on the intriguing Outlet Trail. To get to the Dresden Trailhead from State Route 14, turn east (towards Seneca Lake) at the intersection with Route 54. When the road comes to a "Y," go right and you will see signs for the trail and a trail parking lot on your right. Take the time to fill out a registration form—this helps county officials keep track of how many people are using the trail.

You begin the trail by making a steep descent from the trailhead, where the corridor is lined with a scrubby growth of honeysuckle, sumac, cherry and oak. After the trail levels out and you pass under Route 14, you see a large, flat wetland that was once among the numerous millponds along the Outlet. The vegetation, consisting mostly of cattails and other wetland species, is quite different from that on the hillside above.

When you enter a growth of trees, you get your first glimpses of the Crooked Lake Canal on your right (the Outlet is on your left). The original towpath was used for the rail corridor and now the trail. The remains of the canal ditch grow thick with wetland plants.

About a mile from the trailhead, you see the first abandoned bridge across the Outlet. This bridge once connected to the town of Hopeton, settled during the 1790s. The town lost its commercial prominence by the 1830s to the towns of Dresden and Penn Yan and eventually vanished. In a half-mile, the gorge carved by the Outlet becomes deeper and narrower. The sheer face of dark gray rock with thin, paper-like layers on your left is Genessee shale. If you take some time to look around at the cliffs in the vicinity, you can make out two other types of rock. Tulley limestone is located between the Genessee shale and the oldest of the three layers, Moscow shale.

As you ease around a bend in the trail, you will see what remains of the J.T. Baker Corporation. While currently unoccupied, this site was once home to a gristmill, several paper mills and a

You will see many historic buildings along the Outlet Trail.

large chemical company. At the 2.5-mile mark, you cross Ridge Road, where a flour mill was erected in 1805. A sawmill and a distillery also occupied the site.

When you pass a marker etched with a "D3," it means you have come 3 miles from Dresden. Soon, you pass a huge boulder that doubles as a memorial to John Sheridan, the attorney who negotiated the corridor's purchase for Yates County. From here, you get a good view of the falls at Seneca Mills, which are the largest falls on the Outlet. They were used continuously to generate power until 1958.

Continuing west, you soon pass the best preserved of the canal locks; take a moment to admire its beautiful stonework. The next mile of trail is the least developed section. The corridor is lined with an intriguing blend of trees, with white pine and hemlock on the left and oak, basswood and maple on the right. Beavers are also prevalent in the area near the D4-mile marker.

In a half-mile, you reach what remains of the dam at Milo Mill, located in the Outlet on your left. The most industrialized section of the Outlet was from this point west to Penn Yan. The mill sites are close together and some are well preserved. You soon pass a stone building foundation that stretches nearly 300 feet, giving you a sense of the massive size of the mills. For the next mile, you continue to see many ruins and relics of these structures.

By the time you reach Cherry Street at 5.5 miles, the trail is paved with asphalt and is maintained by the Village of Penn Yan. The village also installed the fitness course that continues for the remainder of the trail. You quickly pass under the "High Bridge," which carried the first railroad operated in Yates County. Just beyond the bridge, you may see some foundations on the right side of the trail and a large, circular hollow—this is all that remains of the turntable that once reversed the direction of many locomotives traveling on the corridor.

You cross the Outlet on a footbridge before passing through a tunnel under Main Street in Penn Yan. Just past the tunnel, you can see a dam on your right that is used to control the level of Keuka Lake. It's hard to imagine that this section of trail once hosted several woodworking factories, a cooperage and a sash-and-blind factory.

After crossing under Liberty Street near 6.5 miles, you pass rest rooms, a boat launch area, tennis courts and a small playground before crossing Sucker Brook on a footbridge. This marshy area is a popular spot for birdwatching. The trail ends after emerging from a wooded area in another village-owned park near Route 54A.

13. Rochester, Syracuse and Eastern Trail

Endpoints: Pebble Hill Road to Pannell Road in the Town of Perinton

Location: Monroe County

Length: 3 miles

Surface: Crushed stone

Uses:

Contact: David Morgan
Director of Parks
Town of Perinton
1350 Turk Hill Road
Fairport, NY 14450-8751
716-223-5050

◆◆◆

I f you are in the eastern suburbs of Rochester, or you want to take a small diversion from touring the Erie Canal Heritage Trail, consider taking a short ride on the Rochester, Syracuse and Eastern Trail.

The route once carried two trolley lines operated by the Rochester, Syracuse and Eastern Railroad. The lines transported people from the suburbs into Rochester. When the trolley abandoned the route, Monroe County purchased the property. The Town of Perinton, which now owns and manages the trail, began converting the corridor into a trail in the mid-1970s. Traversing pleasant residential areas, the trail now shares the corridor with power lines.

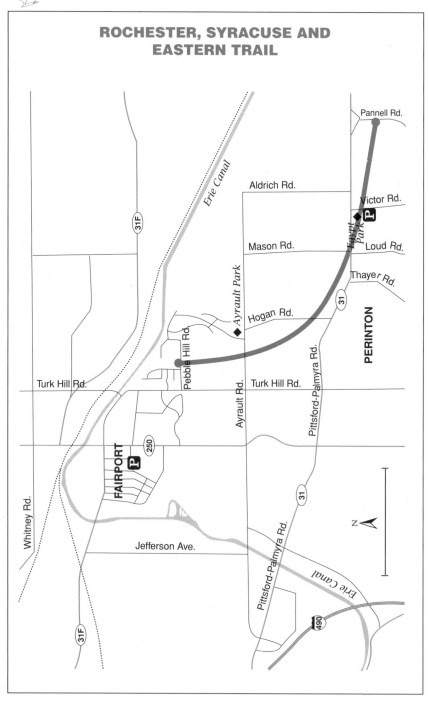

ROCHESTER, SYRACUSE AND
EASTERN TRAIL

Pannell Rd.

Erie Canal

Aldrich Rd.

31F

Victor Rd.

Mason Rd.

Egypt Park

Loud Rd.

Ayrault Park

Thayer Rd.

Hogan Rd.

31

Pebble Hill Rd.

PERINTON

Turk Hill Rd.

Ayrault Rd.

Turk Hill Rd.

Pittsford-Palmyra Rd.

FAIRPORT

250

31

Whitney Rd.

N

Jefferson Ave.

Pittsford-Palmyra Rd.

Erie Canal

31F

490

This trail is a short and pleasant diversion located in the suburbs of Rochester.

The Rochester, Syracuse and Eastern Trail is easily accessible from downtown Fairport and the Erie Canal Heritage Trail (see page 25). From downtown, where on-street parking is available, you are about 1.5 miles from the start of the trail. To get there, head south on Main Street and turn left on Winding Brook Drive. Jog right and then left across busy Turk Hill Road, continuing on Parkland Drive on the other side. Turn right onto Bradford Hill Road, and when this street ends in a couple of blocks, you can see the trail just to the left on Pebble Hill Road. You most likely want to travel south (to the right) because the trail ends a short distance to the north, just shy of the Erie Canal.

As you get onto the trail, you leave the neighborhood setting for a densely wooded corridor. On the left, you soon pass the original site of the town of Egypt's first tavern, which was built in 1812. While no remnants of the building are visible from the trail corridor, the structure has been preserved. It was moved from its original site and converted into a bed-and-breakfast along the Erie Canal.

You cross Ayrault Road at grade within a half-mile, where residential neighborhoods again surround the trail. Houses remain nearby for less than a half-mile as you begin easing your way eastward. You pass an enclave of self-storage units before crossing Hogan Road and passing a tennis complex. The perimeter of the surface is a bit scruffy in this area, partly because it is occasionally cleared for the power lines that tower overhead.

Before reaching Egypt Park, you cross Mason Road, which is quickly followed by busy Pittsford-Palmyra Road (State Route 31)— use caution when crossing. In the community park, you find rest rooms, tennis courts, picnic tables, swing sets and parking. In this area, you also skirt the edge of Lollypop Farm Park, which is the Humane Society for Monroe County. People are welcome to visit the animal shelter, which also offers a petting zoo.

You can end your short trip here, or you can continue for less than a mile. The trail ends somewhat anticlimactically near a power sub-station at Pannell Road, just west of the Monroe-Wayne County line.

14. Sullivan County Trail

Endpoints: Wurtsboro to Westbrookville

Location: Sullivan County

Length: 5.5 miles

Surface: Gravel and dirt

Uses:

Contact: Dennis Hewston
Sullivan County Rails to Trails
195 Lake Louise Marie Road
Rock Hill, NY 12715
914-796-2100, ext. 212 or 561

◆◆◆

Sullivan County, home to the Catskill Mountains, is a quiet place—a pleasant spot to escape from the rigors of the urban environment that surrounds so much of New York City. And tucked along the eastern edge of the county is a short but wonderful rail-trail that follows a wildlife preserve.

The 5.5-mile Sullivan County Trail is part of a county-wide trail network sponsored by the volunteer group called Sullivan County Rails to Trails. The group's ultimate goal is to open 44 miles of trails that will encircle much of the county. In addition to the 5.5 miles between Wurtsboro and Westbrookville, the volunteers have opened a 3-mile segment between Woodridge and Hurleyville. Both segments are built on a former New York, Ontario and Western Railroad line, but are not yet continuous. The old O&W line primarily provided passenger service, transporting people from New York City into the many Catskill Mountain resorts in the county.

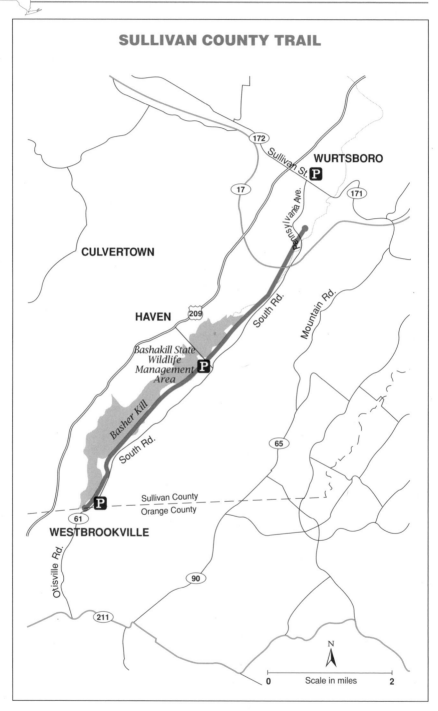

SULLIVAN COUNTY TRAIL

WURTSBORO

CULVERTOWN

HAVEN

Bashakill State
Wildlife
Management
Area

Basher Kill

South Rd.

Sullivan St.

Pennsylvania Ave.

South Rd.

Mountain Rd.

Sullivan County
Orange County

WESTBROOKVILLE

Otisville Rd.

N

Scale in miles

0   2

To get to Wurtsboro from the New York City metropolitan area, take Interstate 87 to U.S. Route 6 and State Route 17. Northwest of Interstate 84, stay on Route 17 west and follow it all the way into the Catskills of Sullivan County. Take the Wurtsboro/High View Exit (#114), and turn left onto Route 171. Proceed less than 2 miles into the quaint downtown area, where you may want to park your car. The trail begins 1 mile from downtown. To get there, turn right on Pennsylvania Avenue (a monument to Vietnam Prisoners of War is located here) and proceed 0.7 miles. Here, the road veers sharply left; continue to follow it for another 0.3 miles and you will see the wide trail corridor on the right side.

Most of this trail parallels the highly scenic Bashakill State Wildlife Management Area. You will see signs indicating that you are in a wildlife area almost as soon as you begin this pleasantly wooded trail, which bursts with color during the early fall months.

Within a half-mile, you pass under State Route 17, which is one of the last signs of civilization as you head south into the

Wetlands and mountains dominate the views along the Sullivan County Trail.

wildlife preserve. You begin to see wonderful wetlands on your left and views of the Catskill Mountains on your right. The area is rich with deer and beaver as well as a wide variety of waterfowl.

Beyond the 1.5-mile mark, you begin to notice a marshy body of water known as the Basher Kill on your right. The trail corridor is sunken down, so you may not realize that South Road is paralleling the trail's left side. The views continue to improve along the Basher Kill. By the 2.3-mile mark, you are passing through a parking lot, often used by anglers.

You cross a short footbridge, and on the other side, the trail surface is often marshy and wet—similar to the trail's surroundings. Young, deciduous trees line the surprisingly straight, flat and wide trail. You may catch a fleeting glimpse of a house high up on your left. However, the spectacular views across the Basher Kill and to the mountains beyond keep your eyes glued to the right. A thin band of trees lines the right side, but does not obscure the views.

In another 1.5 miles (4 miles from the start of the trail), the Basher Kill gets even wider and a series of island-like mounds appear in the water. The vegetation on the right has thinned considerably, opening up a panoramic vista of the entire area. On the left, distinctive paper birch trees are mixed in with other hardwoods. You soon reach another parking area and another short footbridge. Take time to stop and enjoy the scenery.

As you continue, water actually surrounds both sides of the trail. In another 0.7 miles you reach another parking lot. The Basher Kill looks more like a lake, as you reach the southern end of this pleasant journey. A final parking lot is located near the 5.5-mile mark and the trail's end. At this point, you are at the southern border of Sullivan County, near the town of Westbrookville.

15. Wallkill Valley Rail Trail

Endpoints: Springtown to Gardiner
Location: Ulster County
Length: 12.2 miles
Surface: Original ballast of gravel and dirt
Uses:

Contact: Roland Bahret
Wallkill Valley Rail Trail Association, Inc.
P.O. Box 1048
New Paltz, NY 12561-0020
914-255-1436

◆◆◆

The Wallkill Valley Rail Trail is a testament to the power of volunteers. Residents of rural Ulster County—and visitors who flock to the area—can thank a steadfast group of trail enthusiasts who worked tirelessly to acquire the former rail corridor and to develop it as a multi-use trail. Today, a dedicated group of individuals continues to maintain this idyllic trail, situated less than 100 miles from New York City.

Originally operated by the Wallkill Valley Railroad, this route serviced many farms and small commercial enterprises throughout the Wallkill Valley. It also provided passenger service to some of the mountain resorts in the area. The line was actually abandoned by Conrail and purchased by a non-profit organization called the Trust for Public Land, which in turn sold it to the town of New Paltz and the Wallkill Valley Land Trust.

Because the trail was developed as a local resource, virtually no parking has been established for out-of-town users. Do not park

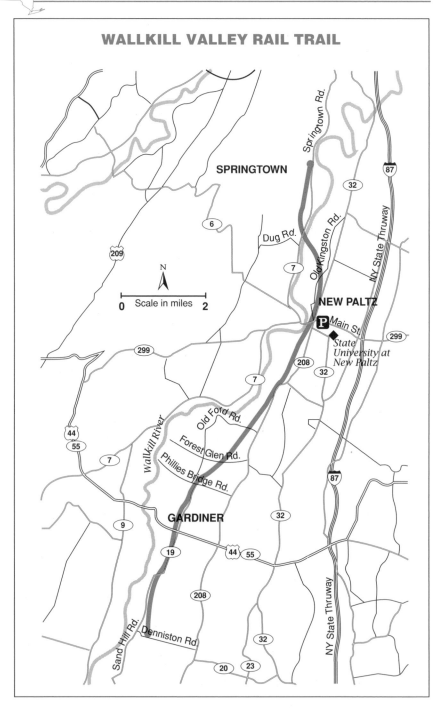

WALLKILL VALLEY RAIL TRAIL

Karen-Lee Ryan

An apple orchard lines the Wallkill Valley Trail just east of the New Paltz/Gardiner border.

on private property surrounding the trail. Instead, plan to find a parking space in the quaint downtown area of the Village of New Paltz, which bustles with bookstores, restaurants and a mix of shops. To get to there, take Exit 18/New Paltz from Interstate 87 (New York State Thruway) and travel west on State Route 299 (Main Street) into downtown. To reach the trail, continue a short distance on Main Street until it intersects the trail after the junction of Route 208 and before crossing the Wallkill River.

If you begin the trail from Main Street in downtown New Paltz, you are about 8 miles from the southern endpoint at Denniston Road and less than 4 miles from the northern end at Springtown Road. The trail surface through town is a little choppy, although it smooths out in both directions.

Heading north on the Wallkill Valley Trail, you face a series of road crossings as the trail traverses the historic district of New Paltz. First, you pass a train station—now a fitness center—on the left side of the trail. Next, you cross North Front Street, followed by Broadhead Avenue, formerly the site of a cannery and the New Paltz Creamery. Today, it is home to the Huguenot Historical Society, where some parking is available. Soon you cross Mulberry

Karen-Lee Ryan

This beautifully designed bridge offers plenty of places to sit and enjoy the views of the Wallkill River.

Street, where you can take a detour to Huguenot Street, one of the oldest streets in America. Turn left to reach Huguenot, where you can tour several 17th and 18th century museum-like homes.

Back on the trail, you see two original stone whistle posts on the trail corridor just beyond Mulberry Street. These posts once signaled train engineers to sound their whistles as they entered town. Huguenot Street crosses the trail 1.3 miles from Main Street and is the last of the street crossings in New Paltz. The next stretch of trail offers a serene setting, with young hardwoods lining the left side. Within a mile, you reach a multi-trestled span over the Wallkill River, one of your first opportunities to view the trail's namesake.

The trail begins to narrow beyond the bridge, and in less than a half-mile you pass a horse farm. Rural agricultural land soon dominates the corridor, which gets progressively narrower. The trail ends at the New Paltz town line, about 4 miles from Main Street in New Paltz. Plan to retrace your steps through town to continue south on the trail.

On the south side of New Paltz, you pass sporadic out-croppings of shale along your right as the trail quickly takes on a rural tone. Birds are plentiful in the area, flitting in and out of woods that include many black locust trees. Less than 2 miles from Main Street, you cross over Plattekill Creek. Soon, the views on your right open up suddenly, revealing the breathtaking Shawangunk Mountains, which were formed an estimated 400 million years ago. A bench is perfectly situated here for viewing and relaxation.

An apple orchard lines your right side as you approach the southern end of the town of New Paltz. Old Ford Road (a mile from Plattekill Creek) is the first road crossing in the town of Gardiner, where the trail is decidedly rural and generally narrower than the New Paltz section. You will be enveloped by trees and entertained by a mix of songbirds.

In another mile, you cross over Forest Glen Road using a short bridge span. The trail is densely wooded in this section of Gardiner, with elm, beech, aspen, sugar maple and tulip trees. You may see rabbits and chipmunks scurrying across the trail. Aside from an occasional house, you see few signs of civilization until you emerge at Routes 44 and 55, where an antique shop occupies an old railroad depot. Two restaurants are also nearby on this main thoroughfare through Gardiner.

After you cross this busy road at grade, you return to the trail's more characteristic rural setting. In a little more than a mile, you cross Sand Hill Road. You know you are in the final stretch when the trail widens to a two-track, with grass growing in the center of the trail. Some nearby farmers use the corridor to access their land, which amplifies the trail's road-like quality. The trail ends somewhat abruptly at Denniston Road, which is the southern border of the town of Gardiner.

16. Warren County Bikeway

Endpoints: Lake George to Queensbury

Location: Warren County

Length: 8 miles of a 10-mile trail is on abandoned rail corridor

Surface: Asphalt

Uses:

Contact: Patrick Beland, Director
Division of Parks and Recreation
County of Warren
261 Main Street
Warrensburg, NY 12885
518-623-5576

◆◆◆

If you are heading to the vast wilderness of the Adirondack Mountains, you can take a side trip—just off Interstate 87—to the Warren County Bikeway. Or, depending on your taste, you can spend a couple of days in the bustling tourist town of Lake George and venture to the trail during your stay.

The trail starts in the heart of the Village of Lake George, not far from the scores of motels, T-shirt shops and amusements in the area. The town is located on the southern outskirts of Adirondack National Park, and the trail begins just off the shore of Lake George, where swimming, jet-skiing and parasailing are popular summer activities.

Assembled from two different kinds of corridor, the Warren County Bikeway has its roots in both a trolley line and a railroad line. Routes orginally used by the Hudson Valley Trolley and the Delaware and Hudson Railroad were combined to form this trail, which opened in 1978.

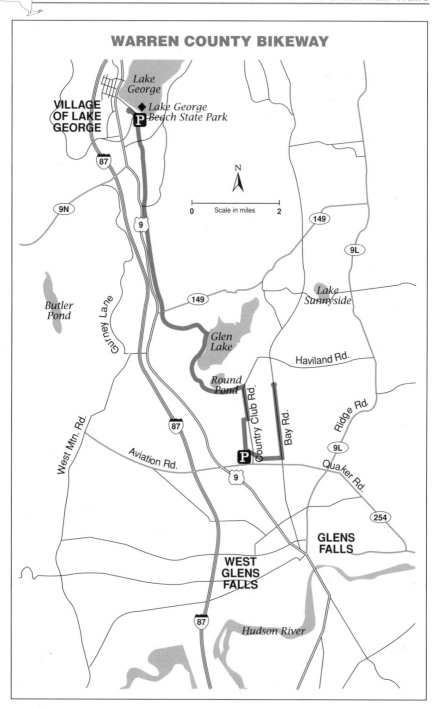

WARREN COUNTY BIKEWAY

Lake
George

VILLAGE
OF LAKE
GEORGE

◆ Lake George
Beach State Park

P

87

9N

9

N

0   Scale in miles   2

149

9L

Butler
Pond

Gurney Lane

149

Lake
Sunnyside

Glen
Lake

Haviland Rd.

Round
Pond

Country Club Rd.

Bay Rd.

Ridge Rd.

87

West Mtn. Rd.

P

9L

Aviation Rd.

9

Quaker Rd.

254

GLENS
FALLS

WEST
GLENS
FALLS

87

Hudson River

To get to the trail, take U.S. Route 9 (Canada Street) from Interstate 87 into the Village of Lake George. Turn east on McGillis, and you will immediately see the lake on your left. Proceed 0.4 miles, past Fort William Henry—where *Last of the Mohicans* was filmed—and turn right onto one-way Westbrook Street. You should see signs for the Warren County Bikeway and for Lake George Park; you can park on-street anywhere in the area.

As you begin the trail, you ascend a fairly steep hill for the first 2 miles. You pass a picnic site before entering a wooded area filled with the fragrant scent of pine. Shelves of rock, strewn with moss, line the right side, and wild ferns sprout all over. Beyond the half-mile mark, you cross a bridge, where you can see the foothills of the Adirondacks to your left.

Within a mile, the trail comes to a T; veer left and the trail resumes shortly. As you continue uphill toward the 2-mile mark, you pass a small amusement park off to the left, followed soon by a couple of motels, campgrounds and other tourist attractions. For the next half-mile, the trail passes through an open area with power lines overhead.

Wetlands are a common sight near the mid-point of the Warren County Bikeway.

Soon you are back in the woods, and a creek ripples off to the right. You can take a break at a grassy expanse with picnic tables before you have traveled 3 miles. As you begin a welcome descent, notice the rocky outcroppings (some topping 30 feet) to your left. After you cross a short bridge, the creek reappears on your left.

This section of trail is peaceful, and the thousands of ferns blanketing each side of the trail give it a tropical feeling. Soon you can take a short side path up to Colonel William's monument. This is followed by a steep, half-mile decline, which bottoms out at a very busy road, so use caution.

Beyond the 4.5-mile mark, power lines resume, opening up a spectacular view of wetlands off to the right and mountains beyond. For a short stretch, power line poles bisect the trail. Many youngsters like to weave in and out of them, making for an interesting diversion before another steep climb. You will see Glen Lake on your way up.

At the 5-mile mark, you come to another T on the trail, this one signaling a 1.5-mile detour. Take the road to the right for 0.4 miles and turn left on Birdsall Road. You cut through the Glens Falls Country Club golf course. In less than a mile, turn right onto the newly-paved Country Club Drive, and soon the bikepath resumes on your right.

After a total of 7.5 miles, you pass the southern parking lot of the Warren County Bikeway. You can continue less than a half-mile on the trail, before reaching the intersection of Woodvale and Glenwood Avenues. From here, you can take an on-street bike route for another 3.5 miles to reach Glens Falls. Follow the green "Bike Route" signs if you plan to continue toward town. The County plans to extend the trail on the former rail corridor another 2 miles to eventually connect with the Glens Falls Feeder Canal (see page 41).

Connecticut's Great Rail-Trails

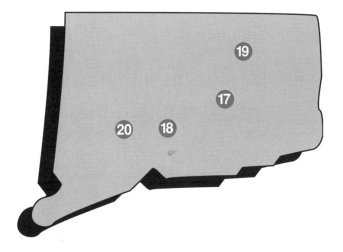

17. Airline State Park Trail (South)
18. Farmington Canal Linear State Park Trail
19. Hop River State Park Trail
20. Larkin Bridle Path

Equestrians make up one of the largest user groups of the Airline Trail.

17. Airline State Park Trail (Southern Section)

Endpoints: Bull Hill Road in Colchester Township to Smith Street in East Hampton

Location: New London and Middlesex Counties

Length: 5 miles (will be 22.5 miles when completed)

Surface: Original ballast ranging from gravel to golf-ball-sized rocks

Uses:

Contact: Joseph Hickey, State Park Planner
Department of Environmental Protection
Bureau of Outdoor Recreation
79 Elm Street
Hartford, CT 06106-1632
860-424-3200

Someday, the state of Connecticut may have the opportunity to boast a continuous 50-mile trail on a former railroad corridor that was known as "The Air-Line" because it transported passengers so quickly between New York and Boston. While much of the land is in public ownership (the northern section was acquired in the 1960s and the southern section was acquired in the 1970s), dozens of impassable bridges have stalled trail development for many years. However, the future holds promise; funding has been secured for further development of some sections of the trail. Visiting this tiny stretch of trail—which includes two hidden (and extremely intriguing) viaducts—underscores

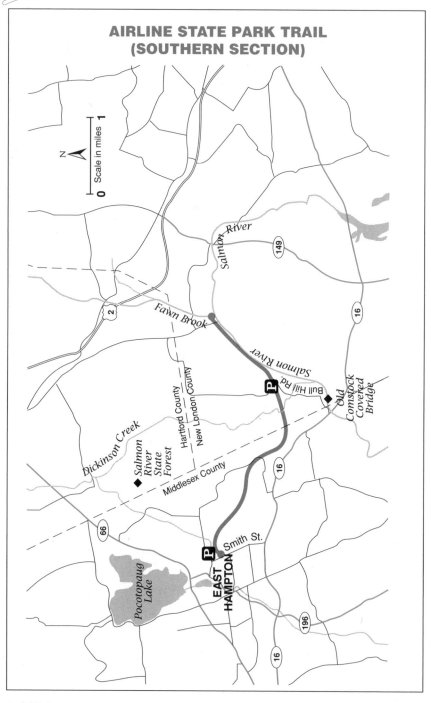

AIRLINE STATE PARK TRAIL (SOUTHERN SECTION)

the extraordinary treasures waiting to be discovered along the Airline Trail when it is fully developed.

The New York and Boston Railroad Company started developing the railroad line between Boston and New York, although the Boston and New York Airline Railroad actually completed the line. Dozens of bridges and viaducts were constructed to span the rivers and valleys in central Connecticut. Two massive viaducts (each more than 1,000 feet long) were built near East Hampton in the early 1870s. Eventually, they could not support the weight of heavier train loads and early this century they were completely filled in with rock. If you take a trip on the Airline today, you have the opportunity to hike, bike, ski or ride horseback across the tops of these buried viaducts.

To get to the developed portion of the Airline State Park, take Exit 16 from State Route 2 (southeast of Hartford) and head south on State Route 149 to State Route 16 (Middletown Road). Travel west on 16 for about 2 miles and turn right onto Comstock Bridge Road. You pass a covered bridge before turning right where a sign directs you to Bull Hill. Go uphill 1.2 miles (passing one set of yellow gates) to a parking area that can accommodate about a dozen cars.

Head to the left, navigating around some large boulders and a gate, to get onto the trail in the direction of the viaducts. The trail is densely wooded initially, but within 0.2 miles, it begins to open up as you approach the Lyman Viaduct. You know you are crossing the viaduct when huge chunks of ballast cover the trail's surface. This surface is more conducive to hiking and horseback riding than to mountain biking, but if you are riding, plan to walk your bike. This mound of ballast and gravel—spanning about 1,100 feet—towers more than 150 high and 50 feet wide.

While the views of rolling hills and valleys off to your left may seem breathtaking, seeing a strip of rusted metal emerging from the trail surface will literally take your breath away. When you see this, you quickly comprehend that you are standing on the top of a bridge filled with gravel and ballast. Take some time to make your way across the viaduct so that you can fully absorb the scenery, and try to visualize what the viaduct below you must have looked like at one time.

As you continue east, you may realize that you are still traveling on a surface filled in by the railroad. The next mile is densely wooded with an occasional rocky cut on either side. These rocky areas are havens for wild ferns and a variety of mosses. Several horse trails traverse the Airline, which is a popular spot for equestrians. The surface remains relatively rough, and you are traveling slightly uphill.

About a mile from Lyman's Viaduct, you cut through an extensive rocky outcropping, which the railroad's developers likely bored through to gain passage. Shortly after that, you reach the Rapallo Viaduct, second of the covered viaducts. This one is longer and narrower than the first. You do not get the same sensation of towering above your surroundings on this viaduct, but it is still intriguing to cross. The surface is again made up of sharp chunks of ballast.

On the opposite side of this nearly 1,400-foot-long viaduct, you can continue on the trail for more than a mile to Smith Street. You pass some wetlands on the right side, and soon a small creek gurgles on your left. The surface is generally chunky, and sporadically sandy all the way to Smith Street, with some sections choppier than others. A pond on your right side indicates that you are approaching Smith Street. Parking is available on the shores of the pond. While the trail continues into downtown East Hampton, it gets progressively narrower and more difficult to proceed. In addition, several bridges near town are not passable. The best bet is to turn around and enjoy the rolling hills and viaducts one more time.

If you have time, it is worth exploring the trail on the opposite side of the Bull Hill parking area. After backtracking to the parking area, you can continue west on the Airline Trail for nearly 2 miles.

The trail on this side is relatively wide and raised up on a ridge. You soon pass the first in a series of rocky outcroppings on your left. Within a half-mile, you can see a waterfall, and you may notice that you are heading downhill. The wooded trail offers a mix of coniferous and deciduous trees interspersed with walls of rock.

Within a mile, the surface becomes quite sandy, which is barely noticeable—until you are traveling back to your car. Soon you hear the rush of the Salmon River below you, which you can occasionally see off to your right. You are skirting the edge of the Salmon River State Forest. Before the 2-mile mark, you reach a bridge that is fenced off, effectively ending your journey on the Airline State Park Trail.

Taking a stroll across the intriguing Lyman Viaduct is a popular weekend activity.

Karen-Lee Ryan

Families flock to the Farmington Canal, especially on warm weeknights.

18. Farmington Canal Linear State Park Trail

Endpoints: Cheshire to Hamden

Location: New Haven County

Length: 6 miles (will be 22 miles when completed)

Surface: Asphalt

Uses:

Contact: John Thompson
Manager of Transportation Engineering
or Vince McDermott
Vice President of Landscape Architecture
Milone & MacBroom, Inc.
716 South Main Street
Cheshire, CT 06410
203-271-1773

Bob Ceccolini, Director
Parks and Recreation Department
559 South Main Street
Cheshire, CT 06410
203-272-2743

◆◆◆

Originally New England's longest canal, stretching almost 85 miles, the Farmington Canal has undergone many transportation transformations. The Farmington Canal, which was under construction for more than five years, opened in 1828 to connect New Haven, Connecticut, to Northampton, Massachusetts. Within two decades, railroads had surpassed canals

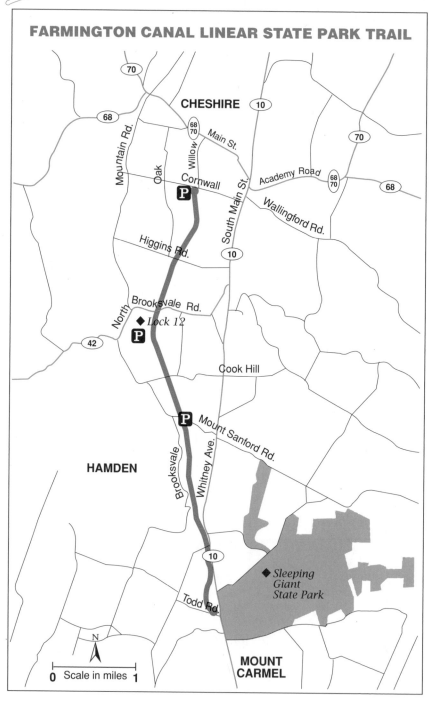

FARMINGTON CANAL LINEAR STATE PARK TRAIL

CHESHIRE

Mountain Rd.

Oak

Willow

Cornwall

Main St.

South Main St.

Academy Road

Wallingford Rd.

Higgins Rd.

North

Brooksvale Rd.

◆ *Lock 12*

Cook Hill

Mount Sanford Rd.

HAMDEN

Brooksvale

Whitney Ave.

Todd Rd.

◆ *Sleeping Giant State Park*

MOUNT CARMEL

N

0 Scale in miles 1

Karen-Lee Ryan

Historic Lock 12 has been restored along the Farmington Canal Trail.

as the choice mode of transportation, and the New Haven Railroad was constructed along the former canal towpath. After opening in 1848, the railroad line passed from owner to owner until it was damaged by a flood in 1982. The state eventually acquired the line and began work on the Farmington Canal Linear State Park Trail.

Since its opening in October 1992, the trail's popularity has soared, quickly becoming the most popular recreational facility in Cheshire. On a warm summer weeknight, you are likely to be sharing the trail with several hundred people.

To reach the northern end of the trail, take Route 15 (the Wilbur Cross Parkway) south from Interstate 91 to Exit 66 south (U.S. Route 5), which leads quickly to Route 68. Take Route 68 west about 5.5 miles to Cheshire, where you turn south onto Route 10. Proceed a short distance to Cornwall Street, turn right (west), and you will reach the trailhead in a half-mile near the intersection of Willow and Cornwall Streets. A small parking lot located here often is full on weeknights.

The trail currently continues south 6 miles from this point. Plans call for the trail to continue another 4 miles north to the Cheshire town line. At the southern end, an additional 6 miles are expected to be under construction during 1995 to extend the trail into downtown Hamden. And, the city of New Haven also is working to develop another 6 miles to eventually create a continuous trail from Cheshire all the way to New Haven.

From the moment you start out on the trail, you will see that it is a top-notch facility, with a wide paved surface, mileage and kilometer markers, benches, solid wood bridges and signs at road crossings that indicate distances to upcoming towns. You also are likely to notice people of all ages using the trail.

The old canal, which in places looks like a wetland, lines the corridor's left side. It is hard to imagine that this narrow band of water was once a powerful force in America's early transportation network. Now just a few feet across, the canal once spanned more than 30 feet, enabling large barges to pass through its waters. Today, ducks, geese and turtles are the canal's primary users.

At the 1-mile mark, you cross Higgins Road at grade. Within a half-mile, you cross Brooksvale Road and pass by a parking lot that signals your approach to the Lock 12 Historical Park. Recently restored to its original appearance, Canal Lock 12 is a popular stopping point. A small path leads directly to the lock, which once helped raise and lower boats on the canal, and to a small locktender's house. Soon after the lock, Willow Brook begins to parallel the trail's right side.

During the summer of 1995, the trail was extended beyond the 3-mile mark, and a new parking lot was built at Mount Sanford Road (3.3 miles). Despite the construction, this section is more densely wooded than the first 3 miles, and a tree farm is located adjacent to the trail's left side near mile marker 4. Route 10, which has been running parallel to the trail for its entire length, now comes briefly into view.

The next mile is a mix of homes and woods, while the last mile parallels Route 10 fairly closely. The trail currently ends at Todd Street, a short distance north of the entrance to Sleeping Giant State Park. This park—offering picnic tables, grills, rest rooms, as well as hiking, equestrian and cross-country skiing trails—is an excellent place to stop and relax after a trip on the Farmington Canal Trail.

19. Hop River State Park Trail

Endpoints: Vernon to the Willamantic River

Location: Hartford and Tolland Counties

Length: 19 miles

Surface: Original ballast ranging from cinder to gravel to chunky rocks

Uses: 🚶 🚵 🐎 ⛷️

Contact: Joseph Hickey, State Park Planner
Department of Environmental Protection
Bureau of Outdoor Recreation
79 Elm Street
Hartford, CT 06106-1632
203-424-3200

◆◆◆

Like many other Connecticut rail-trails, the Hop River State Park Trail is in various states of development. While undecked (or missing) bridges pose the most obvious obstacles, the trail is generally passable—not to mention highly scenic. Located within a half-hour of Hartford, the Hop River Trail offers a fairly rugged experience through central Connecticut woodlands with several small towns and a state park along the way.

The Hartford, Providence and Fishkill Railroad operated this line from Rhode Island to the Hudson River. The line carried passengers and freight, including milk from nearby farms—some local residents even took the train to school back when the nearest high school was in Willamantic. The state Department of Transportation acquired the corridor in the early 1970s and it has been used as a trail ever since. A recent cooperative agreement with a local National Guard unit helped resurface the section of the trail from

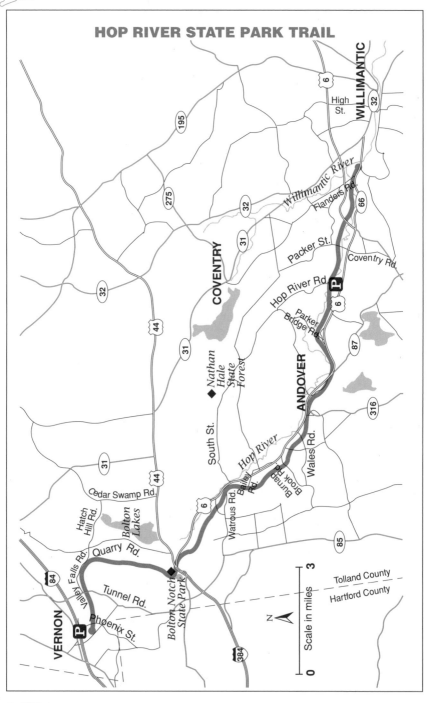

HOP RIVER STATE PARK TRAIL

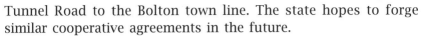

Tunnel Road to the Bolton town line. The state hopes to forge similar cooperative agreements in the future.

To get to the northern end of the trail, take Interstate 84 east from Hartford and take Exit 64-65, which is Routes 30 and 83. Take Route 30 north toward Vernon Center for a short distance to Dobson Street. Turn right, cross over I-84 and proceed another 0.3 miles to Church Street. Turn left, and you soon see a clearing on your left side. This is slated to be developed as a parking lot but right now it is a trash-filled clearing. Do not let this dissuade you from getting onto the trail.

Because many mounds of dirt are in this clearing, it is hard to tell where the trail is located. You may want to continue on Church Street for 0.2 miles to Phoenix Street, where you can see the trail continue on a ridge ahead of you and just to the left. A railroad bridge once crossed this street, so you have to go up a ridge to get onto the trail corridor.

The trail makes a steady climb as you head toward a crossing at Tunnel Road just past the 1-mile mark. Here, you can see cars slowly passing underneath you. Although you will not be able to see it, you are on top of a one-lane tunnel that carries car traffic under the rail-trail. The National Guard installed a new hard-packed crushed stone surface in 1995, which begins just after Tunnel Road and continues for about 2.5 miles. You continue to get ever higher up on a ridge as you begin veering right toward Valley Falls Park. You get sporadic glimpses of Valley Falls Road below you.

Just beyond the 2-mile mark, you can see a pond to your left. It is located in Valley Falls Park, where swimming is allowed during summer months. In this park, rest rooms a swing set, picnic tables and parking are all available—about 70 feet below the trail. You can follow a blue blazed hiking trail, which leads left off the trail, through the trees and downhill to the park.

Rocky outcroppings generally line your right side for more than a mile as you make your way into Bolton Notch State Park. There are no services available in the 70-acre park, however, there is reportedly a secret cave somewhere on the grounds. Beyond 3.5 miles, you pass a pavilion that is on private property. By now the surface has returned to its more rugged original ballast as you continue gradually uphill. The surface is wet in some areas that get little sunshine.

In about a mile, you pass Bolton Notch Pond before reaching a massive concrete tunnel that carries you under busy Route 6. The tunnel often has standing water inside, which turns into a stream after a storm, so plan on getting wet. A short stretch of the trail in this area is a bit trashy, with tires and graffiti.

Once you exit the tunnel, you are surrounded by towering outcroppings of rock that reach nearly 50 feet high and continue the effect of the tunnel that you just exited. Small trees, such as birch and maple sprout from the jagged cliffs. At this point, Route 6 is just above your left side and remains parallel to the trail all the way to Willimantic. For the time being, you can hear occasional cars, although you cannot see them.

Beyond the 5-mile mark, the trail veers right—away from Route 6—and makes a steady descent. The trail remains somewhat elevated on a ledge and gets progressively more wooded for the next mile. Before the 7-mile mark, you pass through a yellow gate, signaling an upcoming road. This one is Steel Crossing Road, and a few parking spaces are located here (not far from Route 6).

The trail remains wooded and fairly rugged for the next few miles. You may intermittently see some railroad ties, and many mountain bicyclists enjoy jumping an occasional tree branch strewn across the corridor. At the 8-mile mark, you cross Bailey Road, followed by an old whistle post and some outcroppings of rock. If you are touring the Hop River Trail on a Sunday, you may hear what sounds like gunfire in this area. Turkey shoots take place many Sundays between 10 a.m. and 2 p.m.

Soon you reach a short bridge span that is passable, but if you want to detour around it, get off the trail at Bailey, head left down to Route 6, where you want to turn right. You pass a small plaza with a grocery store before turning right on Aspinall Drive, the trail's next road crossing. You quickly reach another set of yellow gates and a road crossing at Burnap Bridge Road.

This is about the trail's midway point, and if you look right after the road crossing, you can see the brook cascading down a series of rocks, reappearing on the trail's left side. Known as Burnap Brook, this water reminds you that you are still quite elevated. Fir and pine trees are blended with hardwoods in this fragrant area. The surface here is a mix of cinder and gravel, and the path gets narrower as you make your way toward Andover.

Karen-Lee Ryan

The Hop River State Park Trail actually crosses on top of this attractive stone tunnel that gives Tunnel Road its name.

The trail veers toward Route 6 as you make your way to this tiny town, which is the birthplace of American patriot Nathan Hale. Beyond mile 10, you run closely parallel to the highway, with the trail sitting atop a retaining wall. In town, you cut between some residences and an exhaust company. At 10.5 miles, you reach Route 316, where a large bridge span is missing. You need to go down a relatively steep embankment, cross the road at grade and head back up the other side. Much of the attractive stone-work that once supported the bridge is still in place. You also can get off the corridor here for a short time. If you take the short dead-end street just to the left of the corridor, you will see the town's tiny town hall.

Back on the trail, the views get more mountainous in the distance and the surface gets more bumpy with occasional railroad ties still in place. As you approach Merritt Valley Road beyond the 11-mile mark, you see a tree farm to your left. This road crossing, where an open bridge span is closed to trail users, signals a section of the Hop River Trail that should only be attempted by the truly adventurous. Everyone else should take an on-street detour, or end this trail excursion here.

Beyond the Merritt Valley Road there are five bridges in less than 4 miles. Every bridge has major gaps and no handrails. If you have no qualms about seeing water rushing below you as you try to walk yourself (and possibly a bike) across an open bridge, then proceed on the trail on the other side of Merritt Valley Road.

For those with any doubts, cross under the trail corridor and proceed on residential Merritt Valley Road. Homes line your right, and the trail corridor and thin woods are to the left. The trail cuts under Route 6. When you reach this main thoroughfare in a half-mile, turn right. Continue on the narrow shoulder for about 2.5 miles, and turn left on Hop River Road. In 0.2 miles, you reach a one-lane bridge that crosses the river. If you look left, you see a long wooden trestle—it is the last of the bridges that caused this detour. A parking area and familiar yellow gates are soon located on the left side of the road.

You can turn right to resume the trail, or go left for a very short distance to take a look at the biggest bridge you have bypassed. It's worth a quick look, even just to view the Hop River for the first time. On the opposite side of Hop River Road, you continue toward

Karen-Lee Ryan

Many of the bridges crossing the Hop River are passable—but less than desirable—for trail users; detours are usually available.

Willimantic. The river continues on your right side, darting in and out of view.

The corridor is quite rutted in this area, most likely caused by dirt bikes illegally using the trail. You pass by some corn fields on the left, before passing through a relatively new concrete culvert. You pass under some power lines before a quarry briefly surrounds the trail about 1.5 miles from Hop River Road.

Soon you cross over a very short bridge where the intriguing decking is former railroad tracks placed side by side. As you approach the 16.5-mile mark, you cross under a second concrete culvert before passing an original stone mileage marker. The trail begins undulating again as you travel through a cut in the rocks. Beyond 17 miles, you reach Kings Road. If you continue straight, you immediately reach a bridge across Hop River that is not considered stable. Turn left onto Kings Road, and after the stop sign, veer right to get back onto the trail.

You cut through a third concrete culvert under Flanders Road as you near the end of the trail. At this point State Route 66 is above you and to the right. You get progressively closer to this road as you continue into Willimantic. The trail ends within a half-mile at a massive trestle across the Willimantic River.

While this bridge currently is not passable, many trail enthusiasts in Connecticut hope one day to open this bridge, which would then allow the Hop River State Park Trail to connect with the planned Airline Trail State Park (see page 114), making Willimantic the rail-trail hub of eastern Connecticut.

20. Larkin Bridle Path

Endpoints: Southbury to Hop Brook

Location: New Haven County

Length: 10.7 miles

Surface: Original ballast and cinder

Uses:

Contact: Tim O'Donoghue, Supervisor
Southford Falls State Park
175 Quaker Farms Road
Southbury, CT 06488
203-264-5169

◆◆◆

Just off Connecticut's main east-west thoroughfare (Interstate 84), is a wonderful gem of a trail that is seemingly unknown outside of southwestern Connecticut. In 1943, a man named Dr. Charles Larkin purchased the corridor from the New Haven Railroad and donated it to the state for the express purpose of creating a state bridle path. Today, equestrians—as well as walkers, runners, hikers, mountain bicyclists and cross-country skiers—can thank Dr. Larkin for this quiet stretch of wilderness.

Although this railroad line had many owners, it was originally developed by the New York and New England Railroad in the 1880s. The line ran from Waterbury, Connecticut (once home to a thriving brass industry), to Brewster, New York. The line carried both passengers and freight.

To get to the western end of the trail, take Exit 15 off I-84 and travel south on State Route 67 for a half-mile. (If you need any food or supplies, travel a short distance east on Route 67 and you will find a shopping plaza and a number of fast food restaurants.) Turn left just past the tennis courts, which are part of Southbury's

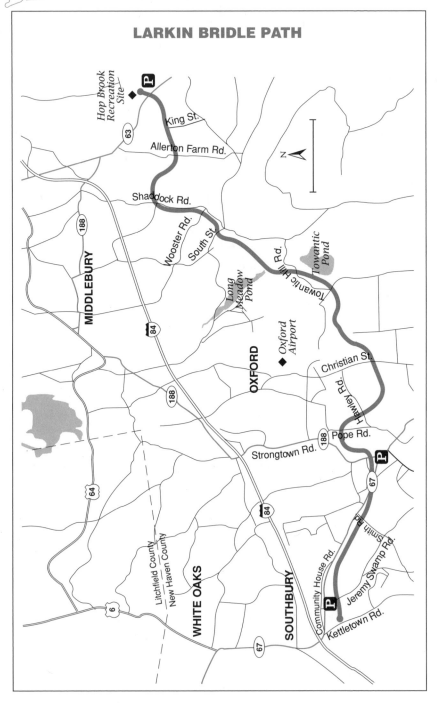

LARKIN BRIDLE PATH

Karen-Lee Ryan

Lined with wetlands and wildflowers, Towantic Pond is one of the most scenic spots along the trail.

Community House Park. You can park here, cross Route 67 and travel 0.4 miles down Jeremy Swamp Road to the Larkin Bridle Trail. The trail's western terminus at Kettletown Road is a half-mile to the right. You can head in that direction or begin traveling east. The trail continues eastward for more than 10 miles.

As you embark on the trail, you may feel pleasantly isolated, even though you are only a short distance from the Interstate and Route 67. Trees arc overhead and an occasional house dots the trail's surroundings. Curt Smith Road crosses the trail a little more than a mile from Kettletown Road, followed shortly by Route 67. The trail for the next mile is quite wide and still shrouded with trees.

You pass a small pond before crossing State Route 188 near the 2.5-mile mark. The Southbury Fire Station is located here, as well as parking for several cars. Within a half-mile, you see some wetlands and a creek off to your left. You may notice that the trail is ascending steadily at this point. You cross Eightmile Creek, after which you reach Pope Road. The crossing at Hawley Road is preceded by a short and narrow uphill stretch—most likely a bridge was removed here.

Karen-Lee Ryan

You will pass through many extensive rock cuts along the Larkin Bridle Path.

Just before the 4-mile mark, you cross over some railroad ties, the first sign of the corridor's previous use. The trail begins to widen at this point, and you also notice how high up you are. There are few homes in this area, although the small Waterbury-Oxford Airport is nearby. After you cross Christian Road, the surface is a more hard-packed cinder and the vegetation is a bit sparser. At times, you get views of rolling hills on the left and an expansive meadow on the right.

Beyond 5.5 miles, you pass through a significant rock cut, where the trail narrows. You soon arrive at one of the prettiest spots along the trail: Towantic Pond. Find yourself a boulder along the trail's edge and enjoy the views.

As you continue on the trail, you need to go uphill, followed by a steep and rocky downhill, to cross the next road before 6.5 miles. The next half-mile of trail is sunk between steep rock cuts and is typically wet and muddy.

At the next road crossing a cryptic sign instructs equestrians to walk their horses for the next mile because of possible danger from sinkholes. Accidents have occurred in this area, so heed the warning. The trail descends somewhat in this mile-long section, although you are still high above most of your surroundings. You pass several rocky outcroppings over the next few miles.

Before the 8-mile mark, you reach South Street, where you can see much of the original stone foundation of a long-since-removed railroad bridge. With the bridge missing, you need to go down and back up to cross the road. On the opposite side, the trail continues to the right of what appears to be a fork. This stretch of trail is densely wooded and the trail surface is a bit sandy.

Soon you enter an extensive rock cut, where trees tower overhead and ferns seem to grow straight out of the rocks. This area has a shadowy, jungle-like look and the temperature is significantly cooler than the rest of the trail during the summer months. This is a nice place to stop and relax for a few minutes. After another road crossing, the trail is again surrounded by woods and you feel as if you are in the middle of the wilderness.

You remain high on a ridge as you pass the 9.5-mile mark. You pass more wetlands, and get a view of rolling hills in the distance. As you approach mile 10, you pass several homes, followed by a town home development. The trail becomes quite rocky, and for the first time, has some trash on it. Next, you see busy Route 63 below you. A bridge has been removed, so if you cross the road, use caution.

The trail officially ends on the opposite side of Route 63 at Hop Brook Lake, where there is a recreation area controlled by the Army Corps of Engineers. To enter the recreation area, turn left on Route 63 and travel a half-mile; the main entrance will be on your right. Picnic facilities and a swimming area are available at this site, which is open to the public from mid-April through the end of October.

Rhode Island's Great Rail-Trails

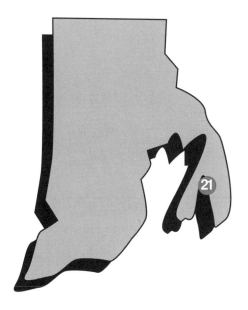

21. East Bay Bicycle Path

The Providence skyline fades into the distance behind you as you make your way to the beach in Bristol.

21. East Bay Bicycle Path

Endpoints: Providence to Bristol

Location: Greater Providence and Bristol Counties

Length: 14.5 miles

Surface: Asphalt

Uses:

Contact: Kevin O'Malley
Regional Manager
Colt State Park
Bristol, RI 02809
(401) 253-7482

◆◆◆

According to just about everyone in these parts, the best way to get to the beach from downtown Providence is to take a quick and delightful trip on the East Bay Bicycle Path. The tiny, but beautiful state of Rhode Island boasts one of the most scenic, well-managed and well-loved rail-trails in the country—the East Bay Bicycle Path. It is well worth a visit.

The corridor was originally developed by the Providence/Worcester Railroad. The stretch of line that is now the East Bay Bicycle Path was used to ferry passengers between bustling Providence and quiet resort towns along Narragansett Bay. The corridor was abandoned in the late 1970s and the East Bay Bicycle Path was developed and built in five stages—the first section opened in 1987 and the last section opened in 1993.

To access the trail by car, take Interstate 195 to Gano Street (Exit 3). At the bottom of the exit, turn left and proceed past the Days Inn to India Point Park, where trail parking is available.

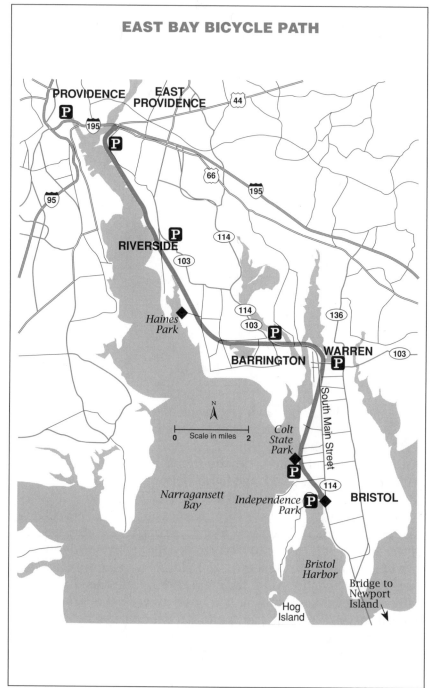

EAST BAY BICYCLE PATH

PROVIDENCE

EAST PROVIDENCE

44

195

66

195

95

114

RIVERSIDE

103

114

103

136

Haines Park

BARRINGTON

WARREN

103

South Main Street

N

Scale in miles

0   2

Colt State Park

Narragansett Bay

Independence Park

114

BRISTOL

Bristol Harbor

Bridge to Newport Island

Hog Island

The ramp that leads you onto the trail (and onto I-195 and the Washington Bridge over the Seekonk River) is directly behind the Days Inn. One note of caution: the bicycle/pedestrian lane on the bridge is too narrow to allow two-way traffic, so you may have to stop to let other users squeeze by. Plans call for major improvements to the Washington Bridge over the next two years, which will likely include a widening of the bicycle/pedestrian lane on the bridge for commuters.

If you prefer to begin your trip on solid ground, you can get on the trail in East Providence just before the 1-mile mark. From I-195, take Route 44 to Riverside (this is the first exit on the east side of the Washington Bridge). Almost immediately you will see a small parking area on your right, which lies directly adjacent to the trail. A map and information booth are located next to this parking area to help you get oriented.

Heading south towards Bristol, water (and boats) will come into view almost exclusively on your right, with the exception of a few areas where small inlets or wetlands line the trail on your left. In the warmer months, you are likely to see Rhode Islanders shellfishing in the shallow waters along the route.

Near the 1-mile mark, the trail parallels Veteran's Memorial Highway for less than a mile. A wooden fence runs part of the way down the road to protect trail users from the nearby automobile traffic. If you look behind you to your right, you see one of the few unblocked views of the Providence skyline, which is quite industrial from this angle.

As you approach the 2-mile mark, a sign indicates that you are about to encounter a steep grade. There is another parking lot in this area allowing people to access the trail. As the trail veers to the right, away from the road, use caution—this is a very steep downhill slope. At 2 miles, water surrounds the trail and the view of the Providence skyline is particularly nice. Old railroad tracks can be seen running alongside the trail here and you soon cross a small bridge.

Before the 3-mile mark, cliffs (and water) surround the trail providing homes for pelicans, egrets, swans and geese, as well as an occasional turtle. The area around the trail becomes much more suburban and less industrial as you travel away from East Providence. You soon approach a residential area where houses line the water. Just after mile 4, you pass through a tunnel under Bullocks Point Avenue and enter the town of Riverside.

If you're feeling a little hot and need a break, the town of Riverside conveniently has an ice cream shop that is easily accessible to trail users. In addition, the town has a parking lot to allow trail access. After crossing Turner Avenue in Riverside, the trail widens a bit (although the surface gets a little rougher), and there are more shady areas along the route.

Nearing the 5-mile mark, the trail begins to feel more secluded, with the surrounding forests providing a nice buffer from nearby civilization. You are no longer traveling alongside the water, although the water is never far away. An emergency phone has been placed on the trail near Sherman Street in case any trail users need assistance and, just after mile 5, another emergency phone can be found when you cross Crescent View Avenue at grade. Most automobile drivers near the East Bay Bicycle Path are very careful to look for trail users; many drivers stop at trail intersections even if it is not required.

You reach Haines Park just before mile 6, where you can picnic, rest, hit the beach or launch a boat. The trail surface is cracked and rough for close to a half-mile after you pass the entrance to the park—in-line skaters should use caution.

After you pass mile 7, you cross another intersection at grade. As one of the many safety precautions along the East Bay Bicycle Path, the trail here (and at other major intersections) is paved in a loose S-curve to slow down trail users and allow drivers and trail users time to see one another. As you approach mile marker 8, wildflowers line the trail throughout the summer and their sweet smell fills the air. Soon the forest opens up again, providing another spectacular view of Narragansett Bay.

As you enter the quiet town of Barrington, you pass Veteran's Memorial Park, which contains a baseball diamond and a YMCA. This area of trail is somewhat rough for in-line skaters. A sign posted here on the trail invites trail users ("Rollerbladers Welcome!") to stop for food and drink at a store just off the trail. Past the 8.5-mile mark, a pizzeria and a bakery also advertise on the trail for customers. In addition, in-line skate rentals are advertised on a telephone poll next to the trail. After crossing the main road in Barrington (County Road), an old stone wall and culvert run along your right side.

Caroline Baker

The wooden bridges between Barrington and Warren are a little bumpy for in-line skaters, but make a great place to fish.

Entering the town of Warren, you cross two wooden bridges, which give you more great views of the water. Between these two bridges, you see an old brick American Tourister factory on your right. On your left, a beautiful wetlands area with tall cattails serves as another local spot for shellfishing.

In the town of Warren, homes and water line both sides of the trail. Past the 10-mile mark, you enter downtown Warren, where you have a number of options for food and drink (including a local favorite—Del's Frozen Lemonade). Trail parking also is available here. In addition, a bicycle shop is located right on the trail at about 10.5 miles. Leaving downtown Warren, you travel along South Main Street, crossing it near Campbell Street. There is a light to indicate when trail users should cross the intersection to pick up the trail on the other side.

Caroline Baker

Independence Park in Bristol, which is at the path's southern, is a great place to watch the boats and rest your feet.

Nearing the 11-mile mark, you pass through a short box tunnel that was built in 1993 to provide trail users with safe passage under Bridge Street. Just past mile marker 11, you get another breathtaking view of the sailboats on Narragansett Bay, and soon you pass through a wetland area where cattails tower over you, forming a natural tunnel. You begin a mile-long, gradual ascent starting around the 11.5-mile marker.

By mile 13, the trail levels out again and small houses line both sides of the trail. At Asylum Road, you can turn right into Colt State Park where rest rooms, picnic tables and a waterfront view are available. Boat launching facilities also are found here. From Colt State Park, you can reach Bristol Town Beach, which is the best place along this route to do a little sunbathing.

At the 14-mile marker, you approach the town of Bristol, and the end of your trip. Here the trail skirts within a few feet of Narragansett Bay on your right giving you an unbeatable view of the sailboats and powerboats around Bristol. Seafood restaurants on your left welcome you to stop and try some of Rhode Island's famous clams and lobsters.

The East Bay Bicycle Path ends at Independence Park in Bristol, where more trail parking and another map and information booth can be found. The park, which was dedicated to Bristol Naval Veterans, offers grassy areas and a short boardwalk from which to admire the view.

Massachusetts' Great Rail-Trails

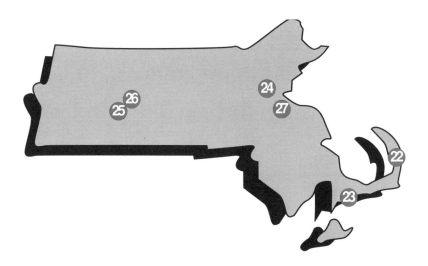

22. Cape Cod Rail Trail
23. Falmouth Shining Sea Trail
24. Minuteman Bikeway

25. Northampton Bikeway
26. Norwottuck Rail-Trail
27. Southwest Corridor Park

Entrepreneurs provide refreshments at many points along the Cape Cod Rail Trail.

22. Cape Cod Rail Trail

Endpoints: Dennis to South Wellfleet

Location: Barnstable County

Length: 24 miles of a 26-mile trail is on an abandoned rail corridor

Surface: Asphalt

Uses: 🚶 🚴 🐎 ♿ 🛼 ⛷️

Contact: Steve Nicolle, Park Manager
Nickerson State Park
3488 Main Street
Brewster, MA 02631
508-896-3491

◆◆◆

Some people could easily ride the flat, 26-mile Cape Cod Rail Trail in an afternoon. Of course, they might not have time to take a dip in a swimming hole or walk along a sandy beach. And they might not notice the pleasing scent of a pine-filled forest or the soothing sound of a rippling creek. And they might have to forgo a visit to one of Cape Cod's quaint villages and the spectacular Cape Cod National Seashore.

You can see all of this and more by taking the time—and a few side trips—to explore the many wonders along the Cape Cod Rail Trail.

The trail follows the route of the former Old Colony Railroad, which carried passengers from Boston to Wellfleet in 1870 and all the way to Provincetown three years later. Train service opened up isolated Cape Cod and immediately brought droves of tourists from Boston. Passenger service ended in 1937, soon after an automobile bridge opened onto the Cape. Railroad freight lingered for another 25 years before the line was abandoned. The state Department of

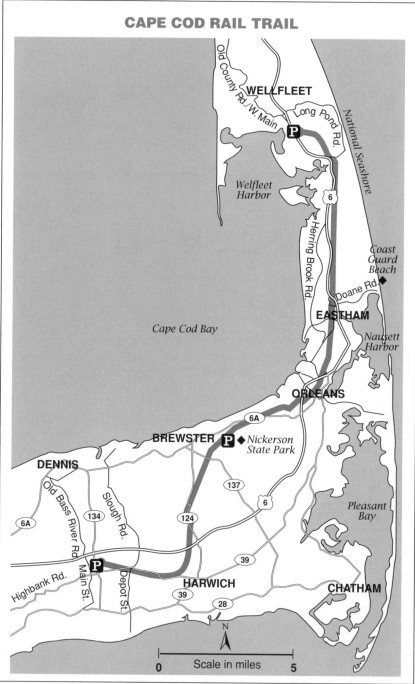

CAPE COD RAIL TRAIL

WELLFLEET

Old County Rd./W. Main

Long Pond Rd.

National Seashore

Welfleet Harbor

6

Herring Brook Rd.

Coast Guard Beach ◆

Doane Rd. ◆

EASTHAM

Nausett Harbor

Cape Cod Bay

ORLEANS

6A

BREWSTER ◆ *Nickerson State Park*

DENNIS

Old Bass River Rd.

Slough Rd.

134

124

137

6

Pleasant Bay

6A

Highbank Rd.

Main St.

Depot St.

39

HARWICH

39

28

CHATHAM

N

Scale in miles

0   5

Environmental Management revitalized the route as a trail, and it now teems with people of all ages throughout the summer months.

A sizable parking lot is located at the trail's eastern endpoint at State Route 134. Take exit 9 south from U.S. Route 6 and travel about a half-mile; watch carefully for the parking lot on the left side of the road. This lot fills quickly, even on weekdays, during the tourist season. A few bicycle rental outfitters have set up in this area to serve the thousands of visitors to the Cape Cod Rail Trail. In this vicinity, you will also find numerous plazas filled with shops and restaurants, so stock up on any supplies you may need.

As you head east on the trail, you are quickly surrounded by various pines, maples and oaks. You also see two stone whistle posts, each with an etched "W," which once signaled train engineers to blow their whistles. Just beyond the half-mile mark, you cross two busy roads, so use caution. The pleasant scent of pine quickly returns as you cross the Herring River and make your way to Sand Pond at 1.5 miles.

Birds are plentiful and a mix of wetland vegetation surrounds the trail before making way for a cranberry bog just prior to the 2.5-mile mark. Within a mile, you pass through a corrugated metal tunnel. As you approach 5 miles, the trail detours off the original corridor onto busy State Route 124 to cross U.S. Route 6. Once you cross the highway, take the first left onto Headwaters Drive, and the trail resumes on the right within a half-mile. Parking is available here.

A 100-year old cranberry bog sits to the right of the trail just past 5.5 miles. It gets its much needed water from Hinckley's Pond, which features a sandy beach on the trail's left side. You can take a break here, or continue a short distance to Pleasant Lake General Store. Offering soft drinks, a deli, ice cream and snacks, the store has been a popular stop since the railroad era.

The 716-acre Long Pond, the second largest freshwater lake on Cape Cod, lines the right side, while Seymour Pond and a welcoming public beach soon appear on the left. Feel free to stop and dip your toes—or take a full-fledged swim. Parking is also available here. You cross Route 124 and soon you recross it, as you enter the town of Brewster.

When the trail intersects with Route 137 (Long Pond Road), you can take a left to enter Brewster Center, where you will find several eateries and a general store. There is a parking lot at the intersection of Long Pond Road and Underpass Road. And, in several hundred feet, near the trail's 9-mile point, you pass the Rail-Trail Bike Shop, a sizable shop offering rentals, sales and plenty of bike accessories.

Nickerson State Park is located at 11 miles and warrants a stop. Here you will find lakes, public beaches, rest rooms, phones, plenty of parking and several bicycle trails. The park also offers more than 400 campsites, but you will need to reserve one several months to a year in advance. Call 508-896-3491 for more information.

The next 2 miles are among the trail's most scenic. Much of the land is protected by the state park, and red maples and black gum trees dot the swampy land that is a haven for warblers, thrushes and red-winged blackbirds. Namskaket Creek creates the border between Brewster and Orleans.

Soon you take a short detour to cross over U.S. Route 6 before proceeding to Main Street in Orleans. Here you can turn right into the town center for shops and restaurants. To continue toward Eastham, you need to turn left onto Main Street—use caution on this heavily-traveled road. It will lead you to Rock Harbor and Skaget Beach, located at the 13-mile mark. After taking in some of the scenic views, continue to the right along Rock Harbor Road.

The trail resumes, following power lines for about a mile. Because of this, much of the trailside vegetation has been cleared,

Long Pond is one of several inland lakes lining the Cape Cod Rail Trail.

making this section of trail extremely hot and sunny in the summer. This area generally is surrounded by salt marshes, and the landscape looks markedly different from earlier sections of the trail. You can also see sand dunes in the distance on the trail's right side. Beyond mile marker 18, the trail is flanked by Great Pond on the left and Long Pond on the right. You may want to take a dip to cool off from the hot sun.

Before you cross Route 6 again, you reach what was once the trail's end, until a 6-mile extension was completed in 1994. If you look to the right, you will see a sign for Coast Guard Beach, part of the Cape Cod National Seashore. A visitors center is located about a quarter mile down the road, and the seashore is less than 3 miles on-road from this point—it can be a final destination or an enjoyable side trip.

The Cape Cod Rail Trail continues about 6 miles north toward Wellfleet. This section is visually less interesting than the rest, in part because power lines parallel the remaining distance and the vegetation is sparse. Most of the development on this end of the trail is commercial or industrial, in between several quarries. The northern end, however, does offer additional opportunities to get to the National Seashore.

If you continue north, you notice that the trail is significantly wider, and the asphalt is noticeably newer. Use extreme caution entering a concrete underpass under Kingsbury Beach Road—it offers no lines of sight to the other end. In a couple of miles you notice an original stone mile marker displaying a 100, and a mile later, 101. By mile marker 102, you are paralleling Route 6, where you will find a couple of places to eat.

The trail ends in less than 2 miles at a large parking lot. Off to the left, you find a fruit stand, general store and post office with pay phones. Across the street is a small tourist information center, where you can pick up maps and plenty of information about Cape Cod.

Not surprisingly, there are still a couple of side trips remaining to conclude the Cape Cod Rail Trail experience. If you continue to the far end of the rail-trail parking lot, you will see a sign to the right for "beaches." If you follow it for about a mile, you will arrive at the spectacular Cape Cod National Seashore. You can also find several off-the-beaten-path inland lakes, where swimming is encouraged, by exploring some of the side roads on the way to the beach.

Take time to enjoy the views along the Falmouth Shining Sea Trail.

23. Falmouth Shining Sea Trail

Endpoints:	Falmouth to Woods Hole
Location:	Barnstable County
Length:	3.2 miles (will be 4 miles when completed)
Surface:	Asphalt
Uses:	
Contact:	Kevin Lynch, Chairman Falmouth Bikeways Committee Falmouth Town Hall Falmouth, MA 02540 508-968-5859

◆◆◆

While you are enjoying the Falmouth Shining Sea Trail, you might think that "shining sea" refers to the brilliant Nantucket and Vineyard Sounds that surround much of the trail. You would be right, but what you might not know is that those two bodies of water inspired Cape Cod native Katharine Lee Bates to write the song "America the Beautiful" and that the trail is actually named in her honor.

Don't let the shortness of the trail discourage you from exploring this historic route that alternates between a quiet wooded path and a bustling waterfront corridor. The trail begins near tourist-friendly (although not overcrowded) Falmouth and ends at the docks where ferry boats depart for Martha's Vineyard.

This corridor was built more than a century ago in 1884 as an extension of the Old Colony Line. A group of wealthy families had banded together to request exclusive train service to meet their travel needs. The Old Colony Railroad agreed and what quickly became known as the "Dude Train" originated. The New Haven

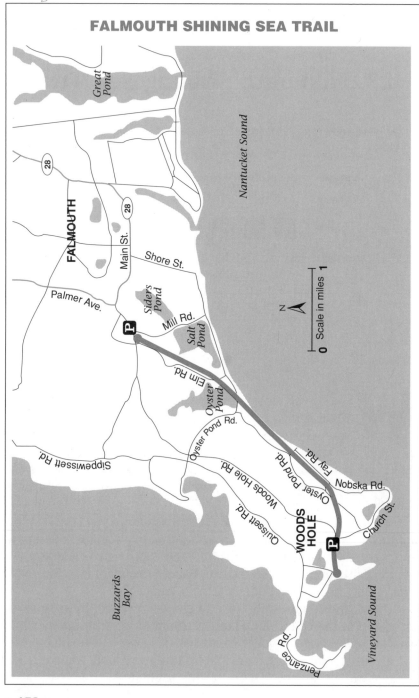

FALMOUTH SHINING SEA TRAIL

Great Pond

Nantucket Sound

28

FALMOUTH

28

Main St.

Shore St.

Palmer Ave.

Siders Pond

Mill Rd.

Salt Pond

N

0 Scale in miles 1

Elm Rd.

Oyster Pond

Oyster Pond Rd.

Sippewissett Rd.

Quissett Rd.

Woods Hole Rd.

Oyster Pond Rd.

Fay Rd.

Nobska Rd.

WOODS HOLE

Church St.

Buzzards Bay

Penzance Rd.

Vineyard Sound

Railroad purchased the line in 1892, maintaining the exclusive service for such distinguished people as President Grover Cleveland and members of his Cabinet.

As the Cape's popularity grew, additional trains were eventually added, although none was as elaborate as the Dude Train. It stopped running in 1916, while other passenger service trains continued through the 1950s. Freight cars persisted for several more years. The tracks and ties were eventually removed in 1972, nearly 100 years after the rail line began.

To get to the trail, head into downtown Falmouth on Route 28 south and follow the signs to Woods Hole, which will put you on Locust Street. Once you are on Locust Street, you will come to a trail parking lot on your right. The trail actually begins on the opposite side of Locust, next to a large boulder with a sign that reads "Shining Sea Bikeway." The planned trail extension will skirt the edge of the parking area and run north from this point.

The trail begins in a wooded setting with an occasional shingled Cape Cod home. Shortly you pass a bench located at Salt Pond, which is actually a depression formed during the Ice Age. Beyond the half-mile mark the hardwood trees subside. You make your first

Salt Pond is the first of many pleasant water views along the Shining Sea Bikeway.

at-grade crossing at Elm Street, where you get the first glimpses of your watery surroundings. Vineyard Sound—and the Atlantic Ocean—are not far from the trail's left side. Soon, Oyster Pond makes its appearance on the right. A handful of benches are sprinkled along this section of trail.

After crossing Surf Drive, the trail closely aligns itself with the ocean. In fact, the trail generally forms the perimeter of the beach. Take some time to breathe the salty air and run your toes through the sand—or maybe even take a quick dip. You parallel the beach for a little more than a half-mile before the trail veers slightly back inland. Plenty of benches line the route for your viewing pleasure.

Soon, young pin oaks and sugar maples line the route again as you meander progressively inland. Near the 2.5-mile mark, the trail joins what looks like a road surrounded by an inordinate amount of parking. The parking lot is not to accommodate the trail's heavy use, but rather to accommodate the plethora of tourists taking the ferry to Martha's Vineyard from the southern tip of the Cape that you are now approaching.

Just beyond the 3-mile mark, the trail and parking lot open up into a harbor where you are likely to see at least one huge ferry loading up for (or on its way to) Martha's Vineyard. One of the best ways to tour the island is by bicycle, so if the day is young, hop on the next boat—just like passengers of the Dude Train did years ago.

24. Minuteman Bikeway

Endpoints: Arlington to Bedford

Location: Middlesex County

Length: 11 miles

Surface: Asphalt

Uses:

Contact: Alan McClennen, Jr., Director
Planning and Community Development
Town of Arlington
730 Massachusetts Avenue
Arlington, MA 02174
617-641-4891

◆◆◆

Steeped in Revolutionary War history, the Minuteman Bikeway closely follows the route of Paul Revere's famous midnight ride in April 1775 when he declared, "The British are coming! The British are coming!" The next day British soldiers followed in Revere's footsteps and the Battle at Lexington was soon underway, assuring the town a place in American history.

The Minuteman Bikeway—named in honor of the Revolution-era men who were willing to fight for their country on a minute's notice—took its own place in history when it was named America's 500th Rail-Trail during the National Rail-Trail Celebration in October 1992.

Decades after Revere's ride, the West Cambridge Railroad opened, providing rail service between North Cambridge and Lexington. By 1874, the line was extended to Bedford by the Boston and Lowell Railroad. The line carried passengers, freight and mail. Exactly 100 years later, a commuter bikeway, fueled by the energy

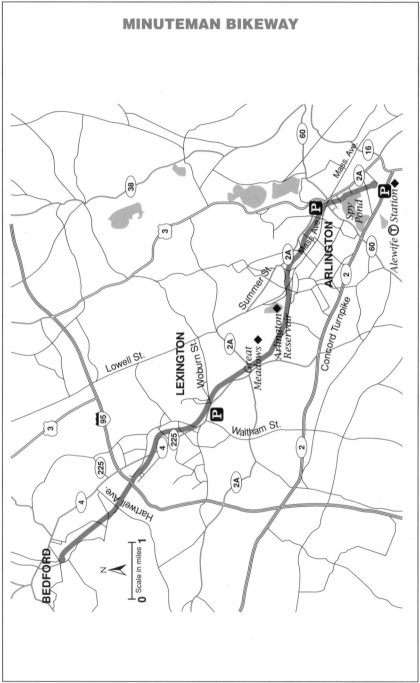

MINUTEMAN BIKEWAY

crisis, was proposed for the area west of Boston. When the Boston & Maine Railroad discontinued service on its line between Arlington and Bedford, the corridor already was slated for development as a trail. Then, after years of delay, the Minuteman Bikeway opened in 1992 amid great fanfare.

The trail actually begins near the Alewife Transit Station about 1.5 miles from downtown Arlington. You can park at the mass transit (known as the "T") station or in the parking lot at Magnolia Playground on Varnum Street about 1.5 miles east of downtown Arlington and a half-mile south of 2A. Many bicycling commuters ride to the T, park their bikes and take the train into Boston. Several trails and bike routes have been developed in this area, and planners are working to link the entire network together.

Many people unfamiliar with the Minuteman's eastern endpoint begin in Arlington, where the trail cuts through the center of town. Ample parking is available in several municipal lots, which are free on weekends. To get to downtown Arlington take Route 60 north from Route 2 (the Concord Turnpike). Travel 1 mile to Massachusetts Avenue, Arlington's main thoroughfare. A municipal lot is located just past Massachusetts Avenue on the right side, behind the Arlington Visitors Center.

If you do begin near Alewife Station, you will see remnants of an Arlington train station—if you are looking for them. As you cross Lake Street, notice the stone curbing along the trail's edge; it once marked the perimeter of the train station. Next, you pass Spy Pond, which provided the Boston area with much of its ice prior to modern refrigeration technology. The ice was harvested in the winter and stored in ice houses along the pond's shore until it was needed in warmer months.

A mile from the T station, you notice an interesting stone structure on the trail's right side. This two-sided mileage marker indicates the number of miles, etched in Roman numerals and read from the side, from either end of the trail. As you face the marker, you will see it has a single line showing that you have traveled one mile. (If you look at the opposite side, you will see an X, the Roman numeral for 10). While these markers can be confusing at first, they add a unique artistic element to the trail.

Soon you arrive in downtown Arlington, where shops and restaurants line streets that are decorated with flags hailing the

Minuteman as America's 500th Rail-Trail. The trail briefly jogs on-street through town, although you can see the only remaining piece of rail cutting in front of the Jefferson Cutter house in the center of town. The Town of Arlington received the house as a donation, and in 1989 moved the house to its current location. Today you can tour the restored home, which sits at the original site of Arlington's town common.

You resume the trail near a statue of Sam Wilson. Born in Arlington in 1766, he later became America's national symbol "Uncle Sam." You pass by Arlington High School at the 2-mile mark,

The Minuteman Bikeway attracts people of all ages.

Karen-Lee Ryan

Wildflowers flourish throughout much of the Great Meadows.

followed by the Bike Stop, which rents bikes and in-line skates. If you are on the trail on a weekend, you may notice people hovering around the Ben & Jerry's Ice Cream window, which serves about 1,500 people every Saturday and Sunday.

For the next couple of miles, you traverse several of Arlington's parks, culminating with the Arlington Reservoir and its summer swimming area that converts to a winter skating pond. Another Arlington park, which is actually located in Lexington, is Great Meadows. It was established as Arlington's watershed in 1873, although the 185-acre wildflower-filled open space now features miles of trails through wetland vegetation.

By mile marker 6, you cut through Lexington Center, passing by the former Lexington railroad station (now used by a bank) and plenty of places to eat and shop. You can also stop at the Lexington Visitors Center adjacent to the trail. Here you will find historic photos and information about nearby Revolutionary-era sights, including the site of the Battle at Lexington.

When you pass mile marker 7, you have reached the highest point on the trail: 250 feet higher than Alewife Station, which stands only seven feet about sea level. Before mile marker 8, you cross busy Bedford Street at grade. By now, you may have noticed the interesting gates at each road crossing. Several unique gates were incorporated into the trail design as the result of an art contest.

Just beyond mile 8, you will cross over Interstate 95 (also known as Route 128) on an overpass. The next crossing is Hartwell Avenue, home to several industrial and commercial developments. The trail passes through a more wooded setting before you reach mile 10. Take a moment to look at the Bedford railroad station and an interpretive sign; a photo illustrates what the station looked like in its heyday. The trail ends about a half-mile later at South Street, where a bakery and a bike and skate rental are located.

Plans call for extending the trail 4 additional miles into Concord, where it could connect to the Minuteman National Historic Park. The National Park Service currently is working to open a bike trail that would run the entire length of the park.

25. Northampton Bikeway

Endpoints: State Street to Look Memorial Park in Northampton

Location: Hampshire County

Length: 2.6 miles

Surface: Asphalt

Uses:

Contact: Wayne Feiden, Principal Planner
Northampton Office of Planning
and Development
210 Main Street
Northampton, MA 01060
413-586-6950

◆◆◆

While on the short side, the Northampton Bikeway is an urban greenway that links historic downtown Northampton to spectacular Look Memorial Park, connecting several neighborhoods and local resources along the way. For these reasons, the trail receives heavy local use.

Because the trail begins in the middle of a neighborhood with virtually no on-street parking, it is best to begin this trail in bicycle- and pedestrian-friendly downtown Northampton. A popular tourist destination, the several-block area of downtown Northampton brims with boutiques, restaurants, coffee shops and a trendy brew pub. In addition, you will find many architecturally interesting buildings, including the County Courthouse and the Academy of Music, which is the sixth oldest theater in the United States. Plenty of on-street parking is available.

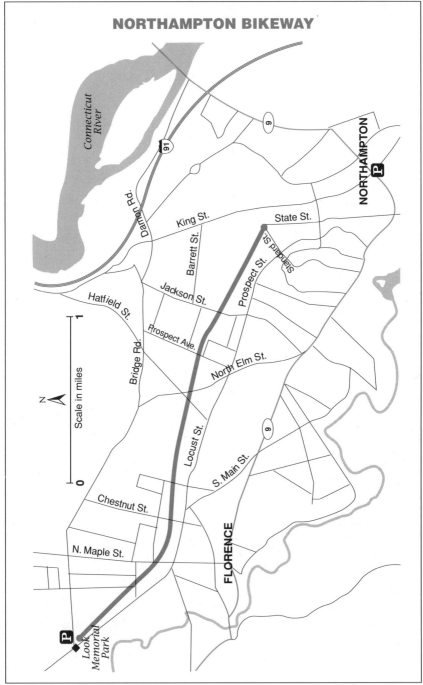

NORTHAMPTON BIKEWAY

From downtown Northampton, take Main Street (State Route 9) west past all of the shops and City Hall. Just before Routes 9 and 66 turn toward Williamsburg and Westhampton, take a right onto State Street and proceed 0.7 miles to the start of the trail. When you get to the end of State Street, you will see the trail in front of you. The path to the right leads directly to a shopping plaza and some fast food restaurants. To take the Northampton Bikeway to Look Memorial Park, go left.

As soon as you get onto the trail, you pass a shopping plaza on the right, while a band of trees shields private residences on the

Local residents are the primary users of the trail.

left. You pass under an overpass after about a half-mile and near mile marker 1, you cross several roads at grade—use caution.

By the 1.5-mile mark, you are passing through another residential enclave of Northampton, known as Florence. You are also near a local diner. In the vicinity of mile marker 2, you again cross a couple of streets at grade before heading into a wooded area filled with maple, willow, sumac and beech trees.

After about 2.5 miles you come to another road crossing, where the entrance to Look Memorial Park is visible to the left. This impeccably maintained park makes the short trip on the trail worthwhile. Here you find picnic tables, playgrounds, a swimming pool, tennis courts, paddleboat rentals, a concession stand and a train ride for kids of all ages. You could easily spend most of a day savoring Look Park's 165 acres of lush, green open space. If you decide to begin the trail at this end, there is plenty of parking, but the park does charge an entrance fee for cars.

If you go back to the trail, you will see that the corridor continues west but is not really passable. The trail is slated to continue for another 5 miles into Williamsburg before the end of the decade. And, planners are working to link the other end of the Northampton Bikeway to the Norwottuck Rail Trail (see next page). Currently you need to take a series of heavily-traveled roads to make the connection. But when these two popular trails are linked, Northampton will be the center of an 18-mile continuous trail.

26. Norwottuck Rail Trail

Endpoints: Northampton to Amherst

Location: Hampshire County

Length: 8.5 miles (will be 10 miles when completed)

Surface: Asphalt

Uses:

Contact: Daniel O'Brien, Bikeway Planner
Massachusetts Department of Environmental
    Management
100 Cambridge Street
Room 104
Boston, MA 02202
617-727-3160

◆◆◆

The Norwottuck Rail Trail is a popular spot for students attending the University of Massachusetts and Amherst, Hampshire, Mount Holyoke and Smith Colleges—and for just about everyone else in western Massachusetts.

The line originated as a Massachusetts Central Railroad route in 1887, opening after nearly 20 years of planning and construction. Stretching from Northampton to Boston, the route carried both freight and passengers—including Calvin Coolidge, a Northampton native. Boston & Maine Railroad eventually took over the line, which had been plagued with financial problems. Passenger service on the line ended at the start of the Depression, although freight service continued on the line through 1980.

The state Department of Environmental Management purchased the line in 1985, two years after the tracks and ties were removed from the corridor. The agency converted the line into a rail-trail in the early 1990s, and opened the trail to the public in mid-1993.

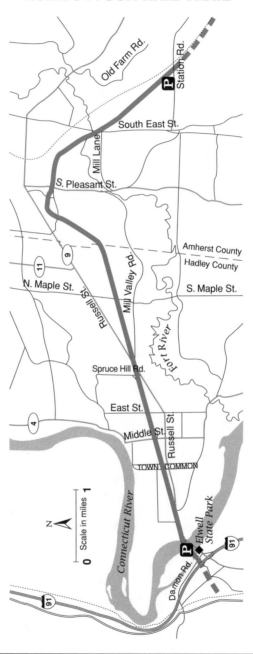

NORWOTTUCK RAIL TRAIL

Old Farm Rd.

Station Rd.

P

South East St.

Mill Lane

S. Pleasant St.

Amherst County

Hadley County

11

9

N. Maple St.

Russell St.

Mill Valley Rd.

S. Maple St.

Fort River

Spruce Hill Rd.

East St.

4

Middle St.

Russell St.

TOWN COMMON

Connecticut River

Scale in miles

N

1

0

Elwell State Park

P

Damon Rd.

91

91

Dense woods surround much of the Nowottuck Rail Trail.

The Norwottuck Rail Trail may be one of the easiest-to-find rail-trails. In fact, there are even signs for it on Interstate 91. From the Springfield area, head north on I-91 and take exit 19. Proceed straight at the end of the ramp onto Damon Road for about a block, and then turn into Elwell State Park. The large parking lot overflows with families and bikes on many weeknights and weekends.

Almost immediately upon leaving the parking lot, you cross the trail's most striking feature: a multi-trestled bridge over the Connecticut River, New England's largest river. As you travel across the bridge for more than a half-mile, you can easily imagine why it took so many years to build.

Below, you can see Elwell Island, a 60-acre preserve that is home to more than a dozen species of birds. If you look to your right, you will see a bridge dedicated to Calvin Coolidge, who served as Mayor of Northampton before becoming America's 30th President.

As you resume on the trail surface, you may notice that it shimmers in the light. The "glass-phalt" surface contains recycled crushed glass from Springfield. You also soon pass mile marker 8; the numbers will decrease as you travel east toward Amherst.

For the next 2 miles, you parallel Route 9 (to your right), while farmland lines the trail's left side with rolling hills in the back-

The half-mile bridge spanning the Connecticut River is a highlight of the Norwottuck Rail Trail.

ground. Tobacco was once a dominant crop in this area and it is still grown in a few places. Dairy farms also served as a primary industry in this part of western Massachusetts, but now only a few farms remain.

You cross under Spruce Hill Road in a short, newly constructed box "tunnel" after passing mile marker 6. Next, you cross under Russell Street (Route 9) using another culvert with no sight lines to the other side; use caution. After mile marker 5, you pass behind Hampshire and Mountains Farms Malls and a few other commercial developments.

By the trail's mid-point (near mile marker 4) the trail becomes a quiet tunnel of young trees—including oak, maple and white birch—while thousands of wild ferns cloak the forest floor. The trail becomes progressively more rural, although the Amherst Golf Course does border the trail prior to mile marker 3. After you pass it, you can stop at a large grassy area where you find a welcoming picnic table.

You are now approaching downtown Amherst, where ramps provide direct access up to Route 116 (Pleasant Street). Soon you see Amherst College on your left as you near mile marker 2. Continuing east, dense woods overtake the trail's perimeter before you cross over the Fort River and South East Street on two short bridges. Much of the surrounding area is owned by the college or the Town of Amherst and is designated as conservation land. You can explore several hiking trails through this swampy area.

Wetlands are visible along the trail's left side in the vicinity of mile marker 1, and a large mix of birds—including herons and meadowlarks—enjoy the surroundings. Soon you reach Station Road, where the paved trail ends at a large parking lot. The trail continues undeveloped for another 1.3 miles, although it will be paved in the future. In addition, at the trail's western end, plans call for connecting the Norwottuck Rail Trail with the Northampton Bikeway (see page 167).

Southwest Corridor Park begins near many office buildings in Boston's Back Bay.

27. Southwest Corridor Park

Endpoints: Downtown Boston from Back Bay to Forest Hills

Location: Suffolk County

Length: 5 miles

Surface: Asphalt

Uses:

Contact: Allan Morris
Parkland Manager
Southwest Corridor Park
38 New Heath Street
Jamaica Plain, MA 02130
617-727-0057

◆◆◆

E very rail-trail is different, but some are more different than others. The Southwest Corridor Park might be the nation's most urban rail-trail. And it is built over five active rail lines: two rapid transit and three Amtrak and commuter lines. What's more, it took hundreds of community participants 20 years of demonstrating, lobbying, and meeting with officials to turn an unsightly old railroad corridor into a landscaped linear park.

The Southwest Corridor Park continues a long tradition of creating open spaces and recreational sites in the Greater Boston area, dating back to 1893 when the state set aside nearly 10,000 acres of land for green space. Today, although the metropolitan area seems more congested than ever, the parks and paths remain an invaluable natural resource.

Until recently, however, one area had lacked open space: the neighborhoods lying just southwest of downtown, including Forest

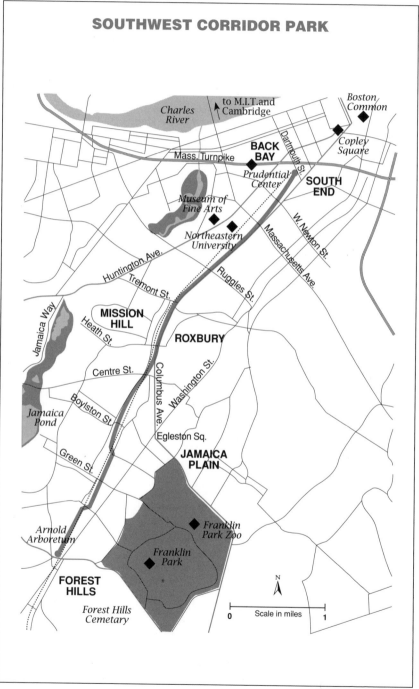

SOUTHWEST CORRIDOR PARK

Charles River

to M.I.T. and
Cambridge

Boston Common

BACK BAY

Mass. Turnpike

Dartmouth St.

Copley Square

Prudential Center

SOUTH END

Museum of Fine Arts

W. Newton St.

Northeastern University

Massachusetts Ave.

Huntington Ave.

Tremont St.

Ruggles St.

Jamaica Way

MISSION HILL

Heath St.

ROXBURY

Centre St.

Columbus Ave.

Washington St.

Jamaica Pond

Boylston St.

Egleston Sq.

Green St.

JAMAICA PLAIN

Franklin Park Zoo

Arnold Arboretum

Franklin Park

FOREST HILLS

Forest Hills Cemetery

N

0   Scale in miles   1

Hills, Roxbury, Jamaica Plain and the South End. In fact, until the 1980s, an active railroad ran on a granite embankment through the area, dividing one neighborhood from another.

After an attempt to turn the route into an eight-lane highway failed, this once-blighted corridor has been transformed into a five-mile linear park with two paths, eight rapid transit stations and nearly a dozen community gardens. Along a corridor that now unites a number of multi-ethnic communities, you find numerous basketball courts, tennis courts and works of art—not to mention two fountains and two street hockey rinks. With so much packed into five miles, it is no wonder the Southwest Corridor Park has won several awards since its 1988 opening. Plan to spend some time exploring the trail and the many historic sites nearby.

A good way to reach the park's northern endpoint is by mass transit. Take a subway ride to the Back Bay/South End station on the orange line of the MBTA (Massachusetts Bay Transit Authority, called the "T"), or take a commuter rail or Amtrak train ride to the Back Bay stop. An outfit called Earthbikes, located two blocks from the station on Huntington Avenue, rents bikes from April through September (617-267-4733). You can bring a bike on the T by showing a Bike Pass ($5 buys a pass for four years). Bike passes are available at the Special Pass Office (617-722-5438) at the Downtown Crossing station on weekdays.

At this end of the trail, the Back Bay and South End neighborhoods meet. These communities were built on land reclaimed from the mudflats of the Charles River in the mid-to-late 1800s, which explains why they are so flat and orderly—unlike most of Boston.

On the trail's eastern edge is the revitalized South End, including the Boston Center for the Arts with its historic cyclorama building, live theaters and galleries. The Back Bay sits north and west of the trail and boasts many of Boston's most notable attractions. Just a few blocks north of Southwest Corridor Park is Copley Square, a huge, two-story mall with dozens of stores and eateries. It is surrounded by several grand buildings, including the neo-romanesque Trinity Church, the grand Boston Public Library and the landmark John Hancock Building. Another block toward the Charles River (and the Charles River Bike Path) is Newbury Street, with its elegant shops, world-class art galleries and several handsome old churches.

In the Back Bay, the trail begins in a small plaza on Dartmouth Street, just across from the Back Bay/South End MBTA/Amtrak station. While gazing at the huge archway into the station, look beyond it for a view of the giant, glass-covered parallelogram that is the John Hancock Building. If you turn around, you can see Tent City on your left, a mixed-income housing development that won the 1994 World Habitat Award. Passing through the plaza, you pick up the brick path of Southwest Corridor Park. A map on a pillar will orient you for the tour.

The first half-mile of the park winds gently through the South End, past row houses, quiet side streets, landscaped terraces and balcony gardens. Soon you see Boston's other showpiece skyscraper, the Prudential Building, off to the right on Boylston Street. Then just before you reach the first main intersection, at Massachusetts Avenue, peek between the buildings on the right to catch sight of the domed First Church of Christ Scientist. "Mass. Ave." is the only intersection along the Southwest Corridor that is not bike-friendly, so if you are on two wheels, dismount and walk across this busy street (which extends for about 10 miles northwest through Cambridge and Arlington). The corridor resumes up on the left side of the Massachusetts Avenue T station.

Soon you enter the working-class neighborhood of Roxbury. Notice that the path splits in two: one for bicycling and the other for foot traffic. This dual-path design is intended to increase use and minimize conflicts between faster-moving cyclists and other users. Shortly, you pass the first of many vegetable and flower gardens cared for by about 150 community gardeners.

After another block, the path appears to dead-end across from a large playing field and tennis courts. Turn left onto the street and right onto a wide sidewalk at the next block, Columbus Avenue. Signs for the Southwest Corridor Park appear after a few hundred feet, just after you pass the field and a Northeastern University parking lot.

The giant entryway arch of the Ruggles Street T Station rises in front of you. One of the eight rapid-transit stations that opened in 1987, this one has a vaulted interior. Next, you arrive at four monoliths, which—through handwritten letters—tell stories of different Boston immigrants who once lived on Ruggles Street.

At Ruggles Street, a pillar depicts a trail map and a short history

Paul Angiolillo

Bicyclists pass by one of eight rapid transit stations along the Southwest Corridor Park.

of Roxbury. Settled in 1630, Roxbury is the center of Boston's African American community. During the 1860s, Roxbury was a major stop on the underground railroad and later it became a meeting place for the newly-formed NAACP. Dr. Martin Luther King preached at his home church in Roxbury while studying at Boston University. Boston's Museum of Fine Arts and the world-famous Isabella Stuart Gardner Museum are located several blocks to the right.

The next stretch of the path contains a small amphitheater, basketball courts and a good view of the rapid-transit lines—sunken behind a triple row of border trees. In fact, one-quarter of the park is decked over the railroad tracks, providing more space for grass, plantings and recreational facilities.

You find more history about the Southwest Corridor Park, including several large archival photographs, in the vicinity of the Roxbury Crossing T Station at Tremont Street. To the right, the recently-restored Mission Hill Basilica, the namesake of Mission Hill neighborhood, towers from atop a hill. Looking left on Tremont Street from the trail is Roxbury Community College and the new Reggie Lewis Track and Athletic Center, built in memory of the up-and-coming Boston Celtics player who died suddenly in 1991.

The next three T stations along the Southwest Corridor Park (Jackson Square, Stony Brook and Green Street) are located in Jamaica Plain, a lively, multi-cultural area. At the brick-facaded Jackson Square station, you can take a side trip on Centre Street to the right, passing some authentic Spanish fast-order restaurants, to reach the center of Jamaica Plain. After Green Street, look straight ahead to catch a glimpse of the minimalist clock tower at the Forest Hills T station—a landmark for the southern end of the park.

From here, you can take a short extension of the Southwest Corridor Park to the left and then along a parkway to reach Franklin Park and the Franklin Park Zoo. (You can find a map of the area outside the Forest Hills T Station.) You can also reach the Arnold Arboretum by picking up the path along the right side of the Forest Hills station. Cross onto South Street at a stoplight and, at the bottom of a short hill, you will reach a gated entrance to the arboretum.

Linear Park Replaces Highway
in Southwest Boston

In the 1950s and 1960s, many transportation experts believed that the best solution to growing traffic congestion was to build larger highways. Boston city planners who had been eyeing a Penn-Central right-of-way since 1948, unveiled a masterplan

Paul Angiolillo

It's hard to imagine this award-winning urban greenway as an eight-lane highway.

Linear Park, *cont.*

15 years later that called for an elevated eight-lane expressway. This extension of Interstate 95 would run into downtown Boston, through Jamaica Plain and Roxbury, with a rapid-transit line down its center. A connecting highway, the Inner Belt, would veer off into Cambridge.

Aghast Cambridge residents were the first group in the city to form an anti-highway movement in 1966. Soon Jamaica Plain residents, not expecting to stop the highway, began lobbying for one below-grade. By 1969, however, the times were changing. Protest demonstrations at the State House persuaded Governor Francis Sargent to declare a moratorium on all highway construction in Boston, and—after intense lobbying from all sides—he canceled the Southwest Expressway in 1972. Instead, a new rapid-transit line was planned for the corridor, to replace the noisy elevated rapid transit on nearby Washington Street.

The local communities had won, which was the first step in creating the Southwest Corridor Park. The community-based coalition that had fought against the highway formed a non-profit coalition in 1974 to help plan and design the park and rapid-transit stations. Each neighborhood formed a task force to focus on its section of the 52-acre park. Community members were involved in all aspects of the park and transit corridor design.

The citizens' concerns were incorporated into the final design, in the form of grade separations, barriers and better street access. Funding was scarce during much of the development, and an $80-million shortfall in 1982 did not help matters. The entire project, including the railroad and transit tunnel, the eight T stations, street reconstruction and park development, ultimately cost $750 million.

Today, it is hard to imagine that Southwest Corridor Park—a multi-faceted, urban greenway that provides transportation choices and recreation opportunities for hundreds of thousands of people—began as a soot-covered, out-of-commission urban wasteland. The result has been well worth the investment.

Vermont's Great Rail-Trails

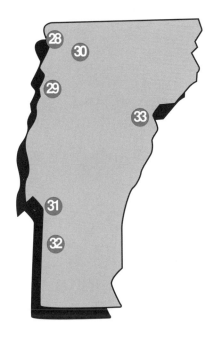

28. Alburg Recreational
    Rail-Trail
29. Burlington Waterfront
    Bikeway
30. Central Vermont Rail Trail
31. Delaware and Hudson
    Rail Trail (North)

32. Delaware and Hudson
    Rail Trail (South)
33. Montpelier and Wells River
    Trail

Goldenrod flourishes along the Alburg Recreational Rail-Trail for much of the summer.

28. Alburg Recreational Rail-Trail

Endpoints: Alburg to East Alburg

Location: Grand Isle County

Location: 3.5 miles

Surface: Hard-packed cinder and gravel

Uses:

Contact: Charles Vile, State Lands Wildlife Forester
Vermont Department of Forests, Parks
   and Recreation
111 West Street
Essex Junction, VT 05452

802-879-6565

◆◆◆

Nestled in the remote, lake-filled region of northwestern Vermont—just a few miles from the Canadian border—is the short and easy-to-overlook Alburg Recreational Rail-Trail. But you won't want to miss this 3.5-mile trail. It is a birder's paradise, with Mud Creek Waterfowl Area on the western end of the trail and the Missisquoi National Wildlife Refuge a few miles east of the eastern endpoint. And, getting to this trail can be half the fun, especially if you take the scenic route (U.S. Route 2) from Burlington that hops you from island to island within Lake Champlain.

The Central Vermont Railroad was one of two railroad companies in a race to reach Burlington in the 1840s. They both reached Vermont's largest city by 1849, before continuing north to Alburg. The Central Vermont corridor continued north of Burlington on the east side of Lake Champlain all the way to Montreal, while the

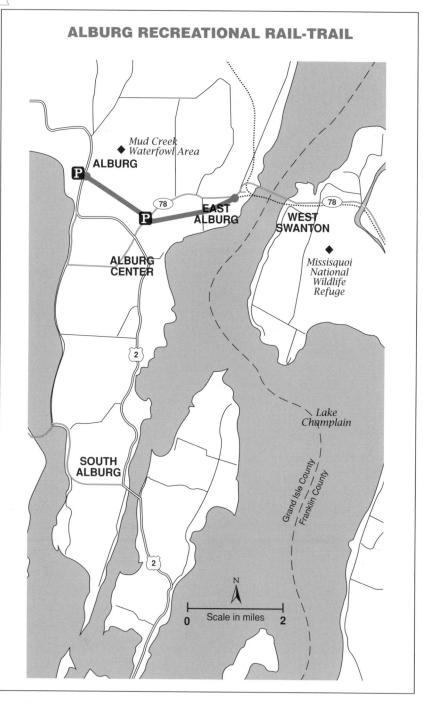

ALBURG RECREATIONAL RAIL-TRAIL

Rutland Railroad took a significantly more difficult route between the islands of Lake Champlain. Rutland abandoned its line in the early 1960s, and Central Vermont followed suit soon thereafter.

To get to the trail, take U.S. Route 2 north 2 miles from State Route 78 into the small town of Alburg. As you enter the town, you will pass the municipal building on the left. Directly across from the Alburg Fire Station, turn right (the only way you can turn) onto Industrial Park Drive. This road ends in a circle, once occupied by a railroad roundhouse. The trail begins left of the circle's center. You can park around the circle or somewhere on the streets in Alburg.

While the trail starts out with a gravely ballast, it turns to a harder packed cinder fairly quickly. You will notice wetlands off to the right almost immediately, where you are likely to see at least one great blue heron. To the left, you initially see farmland, which quickly yields to an expansive field of goldenrod before turning into a marshy, wetland area.

Before you have traveled a mile, the vista to your left will suddenly unfold into a magnificent wetland area. Known as the Mud Creek Waterfowl Area, this wildlife preserve is home to dozens of species of birds—and easily a million cattails. If you are a bird watcher, you could spend hours here. Even if you don't have an interest in identifying specific birds, you still will be fascinated by all of the colorful creatures flitting around.

Within 1.5 miles, you cross a small, rustic wooden bridge that offers a view to the wetlands on either side of the trail. From here, you can see Route 78, which marks the eastern edge of the wildlife preserve. This is a busy road, so use caution when crossing at grade.

From here, the trail gets progressively narrower as you are surrounded by woods on both sides. At 2.4 miles, you cross Blue Rock Road at grade. You can catch some wonderful views of Lake Champlain if you turn right onto this paved road. Traveling a short distance off the trail, you will see the lake, as well as an RV park and a bed and breakfast.

Back on the trail, you remain shrouded in trees, although you do occasionally get glimpses of farms on the right side. Within another half-mile, you cross a private gravel road that leads into a development known as McGregor Point. When you get to a set of railroad tracks, you are just about at the end of the trail, which ends abruptly at Route 78.

If you look closely, you will notice a "Y" shape in the remaining tracks. At one time three different railroad lines came together at this point, and locomotives changed direction before proceeding over Lake Champlain or heading into Canada. The bridge over Lake Champlain has long since been dismantled, but you can cross the lake on Route 78.

If you haven't seen enough wildlife for one day, cross the bridge and continue another mile to the Missisquoi National Wildlife Refuge. Covering nearly 6,000 acres, this refuge is a haven for dozens of species of waterfowl, as well as a wide mix of mammals.

29. Burlington Waterfront Bikeway

Endpoints: Oakledge Park to the Winooski River

Location: Chittenden County

Length: 7.5 miles

Surface: Asphalt

Uses: 🚶 🚲 ♿ 🛼 🎣 ⛷️

Contact: Robert Whalen, Superintendent of Parks
Burlington Department of Parks and
   Recreation
1 LaValley Lane
Burlington, VT 05401
802-865-7247

◆◆◆

Waterfront developments in urban areas have grown increasingly popular in recent years. Judging from the number of people flocking to the shores of Lake Champlain, Burlington's waterfront improvements are a hit with visitors and residents alike.

From the early morning hours until after sunset, people of all ages can be seen enjoying the waterfront beaches, the community parks and the boat docks—not to mention the spectacular views. The best way to see all of this wonderful scenery is to travel the Burlington Waterfront Bikeway. This former abandoned rail corridor and derelict rail yard have been transformed into the pride of Vermont's largest city—all within a couple of blocks of its renowned bicycle- and pedestrian-friendly downtown.

Central Vermont Railroad constructed this line (and several other parallel routes), with the first train arriving in Burlington in

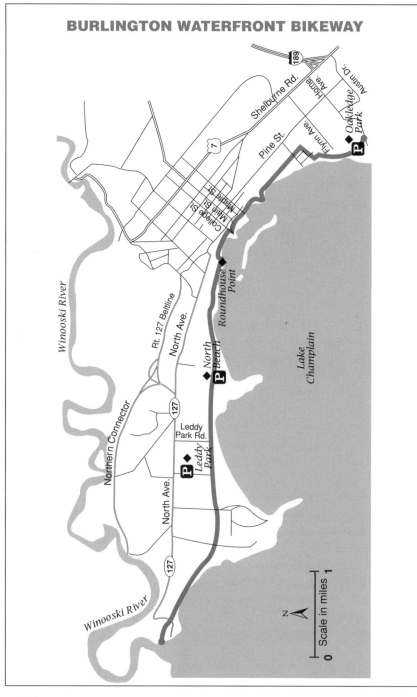

BURLINGTON WATERFRONT BIKEWAY

December 1849. Industry boomed along the route, and within 20 years, Burlington had become the nation's third largest lumber port (behind Chicago and Albany). Although the lumber business went into decline before the turn of the century, the railroad route continued to thrive throughout much of the 20th century.

The city acquired the line in the early 1970s and developed it in sections, completing the entire trail by 1987. Central Vermont's mainline, which links the Canadian and U.S. rail systems, still exists and parallels the trail's southern section.

To get to the southeastern end of the Burlington Bikeway, take Interstate 189 to Shelburne Road (U.S. Route 7). Turn left onto Flynn Avenue and proceed 0.8 miles to Oakledge Park, located on the waterfront of Lake Champlain. This park, where you will find rest rooms, a bathhouse, tennis courts, baseball fields, picnic tables, shelters and a small beach with a lifeguard, is a pleasant place to start your trip on the Burlington Bikeway.

Head right out of the parking lot to get to the start of the trail. As you begin on the path, the shores of Lake Champlain line your left side. Within about 0.3 miles, you veer away from the lake temporarily. To get to the actual rail corridor, turn right onto Harrison Avenue, and travel three short blocks to the railroad tracks. Take a left here, where the trail parallels an existing set of tracks for 1 mile and cuts through a light industrial area, which ends at Roundhouse Point.

For the short distance between Roundhouse Point and Perkins Pier, you find several benches, a picnic area, rest rooms and a boat launch, as well as car and trailer parking. Several sculptures and attractive plantings also line the waterfront along this section of trail. Stop on one of the many benches and enjoy the dramatic views of Lake Champlain.

The trail continues off to the right and weaves through a large ferry boat parking lot as it skirts downtown Burlington. Several restaurants and shops are located here, or you can venture into the pedestrian-friendly city via King Street, Main Street or College Street.

Back on the trail, you continue to parallel a set of railroad tracks before entering Waterfront Park and Promenade. This well-manicured green space was a joint project between Burlington citizens, the State of Vermont and the Central Vermont Railroad.

At this end of the park, which offers public phones and water fountains, you can catch a shuttle bus into town, using a bus equipped with bike racks.

Beyond Waterfront Park, the active rail line veers away from the trail, and the 40-acre Burlington Urban Reserve lines your left side. In less than a mile, the trail heads uphill, until you arrive atop a high ridge that provides sweeping views of the city, Lake Champlain and the Adirondack Mountains in New York.

About 3.5 miles from the start of the trail, you cut through an area called North Beach, where you find a campground, a picnic area, playgrounds, parking, a bathhouse and a beach. This marks the trail's midpoint, and offers a wonderful spot to have a picnic or to go for a swim.

The next mile of trail is pleasantly wooded, with maple, oak, sumac and willow trees creating the green setting. You will pass through a residential area before reaching Leddy Park just past the 4.5-mile mark. Here you will find abundant parking, as well as softball diamonds, soccer fields, tennis and basketball courts and rest rooms. You can also swim or sailboard at the Leddy Park Beach.

Karen-Lee Ryan

In-line skating is one of the most popular activities along the Burlington Waterfront Bikeway

Lake Champlain laps the edge of the Bikeway near downtown Burlington.

Residential neighborhoods resume beyond the park, and in less than a mile, spectacular views suddenly open up off to your left. A small sitting area has been developed, so you can rest while you enjoy the view. If you haven't taken advantage of the beaches yet, an extensive staircase system will take you down to another sandy beach—just remember you'll need to climb back up those stairs to get back on the trail!

Another sitting area has been developed in less than a half-mile. Soon after crossing North Avenue at grade, the bikeway ends at the Winooski River. The bridge over this river has been dismantled, preventing a trail extension into the City of Colchester in the near future.

Karen-Lee Ryan

The Missisquoi River parallels the Central Vermont Trail's western half.

30. Central Vermont Rail Trail

Endpoints:	St. Albans to Richford
Location:	Franklin County
Length:	27 miles
Surface:	Original ballast, ranging from loose gravel to fist-size rocks
Uses:	
Contact:	Charles Vile, State Lands Wildlife Forester Vermont Department of Forests, Parks and Recreation 111 West Street Essex Junction, VT 05452 802-879-6565

◆◆◆

Despite its name, this rail-trail is not located in the central part of the Green Mountain state. The name is derived from the Central Vermont Railroad, which originally serviced the line. The Central Vermont Rail Trail is open to a wide range of users, but this trail is not for everyone—at least not yet.

A rugged sense of adventure is a key aspect of enjoying this trail, which is not yet fully developed. An ankle-deep ballast is the route's current surface and this makes for a bumpy ride. The stunning Vermont scenery, however, may lure people to the trail despite the rough surface, and the first 9 miles (between St. Albans and Sheldon Junction) are slated to be surfaced with crushed limestone during the summer of 1996. Call the manager for details on which sections are under construction.

Known as "Rail City," St. Albans had 17 railroad lines in its industrial heyday and was the headquarters to the Central Vermont

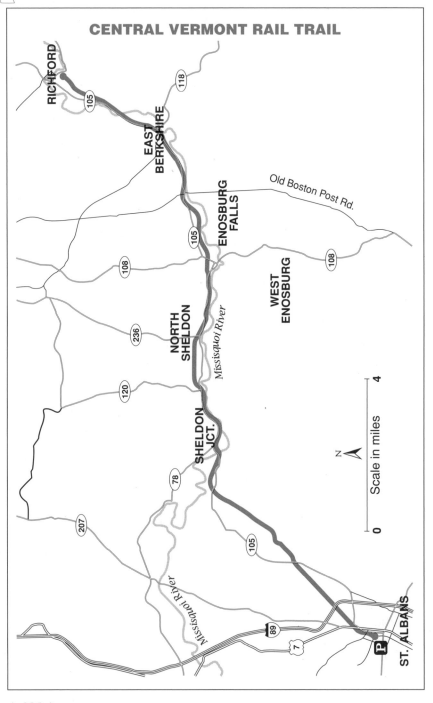

CENTRAL VERMONT RAIL TRAIL

RICHFORD

105

118

EAST BERKSHIRE

ENOSBURG FALLS

Old Boston Post Rd.

105

108

108

WEST ENOSBURG

236

NORTH SHELDON

Missisquoi River

120

SHELDON JCT.

78

N

Scale in miles

4

0

207

Missisquoi River

89

7

105

P

ST. ALBANS

Railroad for a more than a century. However, the city's biggest claim to fame is that it was the site of the Civil War's northernmost skirmish. On October 19, 1864, more than 20 Confederate soldiers led the "St. Albans Raid," robbing three banks, stealing horses and spreading terror through town before fleeing to Canada. In town, you will find an interesting historical museum highlighting different aspects of St. Albans past, including its railroad history.

The rail line to Richford hauled primarily agricultural freight and connected with the Canadian Pacific Railroad. The line remained active until a train derailed near Sheldon Junction in the mid-1980s, destroying the bridge over the Missisquoi River. Ironically, it was a Boston & Maine Railroad train that caused the damage to the Central Vermont bridge; B&M was using the corridor temporarily because a different accident had damaged its own corridor.

At the urging of snowmobilers in the state, led by the Vermont Area Snow Travelers, the state eventually acquired the route as a multi-use trail.

The trail begins near the intersection of State Routes 7 and 105 near downtown St. Albans. Take Exit 19 from Interstate 89 and follow the signs to north Route 7, which becomes quaint Main Street. Look to your right immediately after crossing Route 105, and you will see the entrance to the Central Vermont Trail. The adjacent lot is privately owned—do not park there. Your best bet is to find on-street parking in St. Albans until the trail is more developed and trail parking has been established.

As soon as you get on the trail, you know that you are in for a rugged experience. The surface in many places is quite thick with ballast and loose gravel and demands some concentration if you are riding a bike.

Heading northeast, farmland generally lines your route. The crossing under I-89 signals your departure from St. Albans and your entrance into Vermont's rural countryside. Take some time to stop and look at the rolling farmland around you—it's easy to focus so much on the trail surface that you forget to enjoy the scenery. You will see fields of corn and wildflower-filled meadows framed by a mountainous backdrop.

The trail itself undulates, alternately inclining and declining. You make a half-mile descent beginning just beyond the 1.5-mile mark. The rural Vermont scenery continues for a few serene miles; the

Karen-Lee Ryan

Occasional farms dot the landscape surrounding the Central Vermont Rail Trail.

only sounds are the peeps of colorful birds and the hum of distant farm machinery.

Just prior to the 3.5-mile mark, you cross Route 105 before beginning a steady climb into a Vermont forest. You pass by an area on the right within a half-mile that appears to have suffered a fire and is now a wetland. Just after this area, a relatively young deciduous forest lines the trail on both sides. This entire region was logged extensively during the railroad era.

Near mile 5, you begin paralleling a dirt road, which follows the trail corridor for the next couple of miles. This section remains a mix of woodlands and wildflowers, with an occasional house. Soon you again cross Route 105 in Sheldon Springs, where you find a gas station with a convenience store. The views to the nearby mountains begin to open up at this point, as only a thin band of trees separates you from the surrounding scenery.

You meet up with Route 105 again at Sheldon Junction, nearly 9 miles into your journey. At this point, you see two-thirds of a trestle crossing the cavernous Missisquoi River. This is an eerie reminder of the debacle that caused the rail route's demise. To get around this seemingly permanent detour, take a left onto Route 105, cross the river and then take your first right. Weave your way through the Nutrite parking lot (over some remaining, although unused, railroad tracks) back to the Central Vermont corridor.

From here all the way to Richford, the trail basically parallels Route 105, so if the progressively chunkier ballast overwhelms you, there is an alternate place to ride (although the road offers virtually no shoulder). You parallel some farmland, and within 1.5 miles, the views suddenly reveal the rocky Missisquoi River below on your right side. In another half-mile, you pass a restaurant that offers your last chance to get a bite for several miles.

Before mile 12, you cross Route 105, heading away from the river and into a more lightly wooded area. And, if you thought the surface was rough until this point, you are *really* in for a bumpy ride. Mountains and farms dominate the landscape, offering only fleeting views of the river. Within 2 miles, you cross Route 105 again at grade, continuing to traverse farmland. Just before mile 13, you reach Route 236. This is the trail's midway mark, and perhaps a turning around point for all but the hardiest souls.

At this point the trail (if you are still on it) is surrounded by corn. Mountain biking is truly a challenge, and even hiking is somewhat cumbersome, although the scenery continues to captivate the senses. You will enter Enosburg Falls by mile 16 of this coarse adventure. If you are not already on Route 105, you should get on it for the next half-mile to avoid a bridge with no decking or handrails.

When you get to Main Street, where you will find several shops, restaurants and antique stores, turn right and then make a left onto Depot Street to get back onto the trail. If you like Victorian architecture, you may want to take a quick jaunt through town. You will see an old, unrestored depot as well as an opera house. From here, you are about 10 miles from Richford.

You cross Route 105 several more times in the next section of trail. The views open to the rolling farmland, and you occasionally get some glimpses of the scenic river, lined with willow trees. About 5 miles from Richford, you are surrounded by corn. In another 2 miles, you approach a trestle over the Missisquoi River. Ties remain in place, enabling you to cross the bridge, but be prepared to see the river below because of gaps between the ties.

After parting ways with the river, the trail gets progressively less scenic, and within another mile, Route 105 also veers away from the trail. Power lines parallel the trail corridor before it ends in the town of Richford. At this point, you are just a couple of miles from the Canadian border. Future plans call for developing a trail across the international border, and, ultimately, all the way to Montreal.

31. Delaware and Hudson Rail Trail (Northern Section)

Endpoints: Castleton to Poultney

Location: Rutland County

Length: 9.2 miles

Surface: Original ballast, ranging from hard-packed cinder to gravel

Uses:

Contact: Gary Salmon, Trails Coordinator
Department of Forests, Parks and Recreation
Vermont Agency of Natural Resources
RR 2, Box 261
Pittsford, VT 05763
802-483-2314

◆◆◆

I f you want to escape the hectic pace of most urban areas of the northeast, plan a trip to the Delaware and Hudson Rail Trail. Currently tucked along the rural western border of Vermont, the Delaware and Hudson Rail Trail eventually will be a 34.3-mile trail straddling southwestern Vermont and part of eastern New York state. Despite the fact that the two sections of the trail in Vermont are separated by 15 undeveloped miles in New York, the peaceful and unhurried setting of the D&H Trail makes the trip more than worthwhile.

The area wasn't always as quiet as it is today. The history of this railroad line is deeply rooted in the once-bustling slate industry. The Delaware and Hudson Railroad constructed this corridor in the mid-1800s to move squares of high-quality red, green and

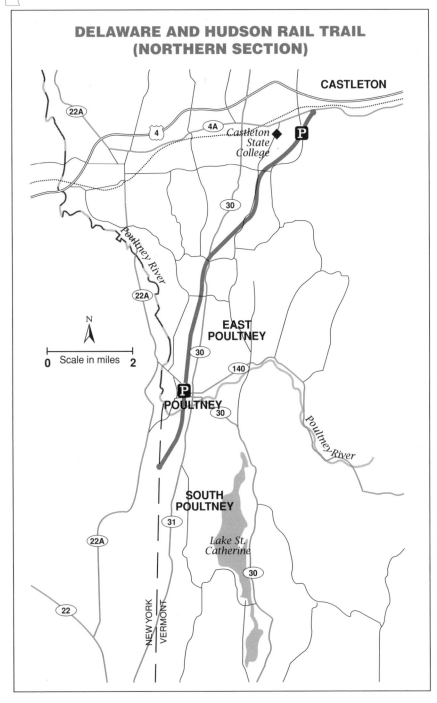

DELAWARE AND HUDSON RAIL TRAIL (NORTHERN SECTION)

CASTLETON

22A

4

4A

Castleton State College

P

30

Poultney River

22A

N

Scale in miles

0   2

EAST POULTNEY

30

140

P

POULTNEY

30

Poultney River

SOUTH POULTNEY

31

22A

Lake St. Catherine

30

22

NEW YORK

VERMONT

Remnants of the slate industry still line the trail.

purple roofing slate to markets throughout New York and the Northeast. The line quickly became known as the "Slate Picker," and in 1890 alone, it carried 170,000 squares of slate from the area. Dairy farmers also made use of the line, as did passengers until the need for passenger service fell off sharply during the Depression.

As trucks gained popularity, the "Slate Picker" suffered a slow but steady decline. The last train ran on the line in 1983. Vermont purchased its sections of the corridor and planned to operate a short line railroad. When that plan did not work out, the state—with prodding from the Vermont Association of Snow Travelers—began working to convert its sections of the line into a trail in the late 1980s. Upon completion of 17 bridges, the northern and southern sections of the rail-trail opened in the early 1990s. Because of the uncertainty of when the 14.5-mile section in New York will open, this trail is covered in two sections (see page 209 for southern section of the D&H Trail).

The northern endpoint for the northern section of the D&H Trail is in the town of Castleton, and the state has made arrangements for trail parking at Castleton State College. To get to the parking lot, head west on U.S. Route 4 from Rutland, and take Exit 5 to

Beavers

It's been said that beavers are the animals most similar to humans, because they change their environment to create their own habitat. These frumpy, nocturnal rodents are enterprising little lumberjacks capable of felling trees, damming ponds and engineering sophisticated canal systems.

Beavers were harvested in great numbers from the early 1650s to the late 1850s, when beaver pelt trading flourished. Millions of rodents were slaughtered until demand for the pelts waned in the mid-19th century.

An illustrious engineer, the beaver is superbly engineered. A flat, rudder-like tail propels it through water, yet acts as a brace for balance when gnawing at trees; its fat and thick fur (which the beaver waterproofs by smearing with a greasy discharge stored in oil glands) insulate like a wet suit; and valve-like ears and nose close off under water.

This ugly duckling that lumbers about on land turns into a sleek swan in the water. It creates wetlands by building dams so that it can safely maneuver around to its favorite food ▶

An obvious indication of beaver activity.

Beavers, *cont.*

sources: deciduous trees, saplings, shrubs and aquatic plants.

Beavers are nocturnal, so you generally only see the effects of the animals along rail-trails. Orange enamel-coated incisors gnaw away at trees that, when felled, are towed and put into place to create dams. A rise in the water level upstream creates a pond. Branches, tree trunks, grasses and mud are woven together into dome-like lodges as part of a family effort.

The ponds are a boon for other aquatic animals, as well as fish-eating birds. At the same time, moose, deer and elk thrive on the aquatic vegetation.

Route 4A west toward Castleton College. After a half-mile, turn left into the college entrance (Seminary Street). Pass several college buildings, before turning right into the visitor parking area. Proceed to the end of the lot; a row of parking spaces on the right side are designated D&H Trail parking spaces. The trail is located adjacent to the row of parking spaces.

You head south (away from the college) on the trail, passing a wide variety of trees along the way, including white pine, willow, red oak and sugar maple. At 0.3 miles, you see a fork off to the left, which is a remnant of an old switching station where trains once turned around. The trail surface, made up of hard-packed cinder, is quite smooth in this area. Farmland generally surrounds the trail, although if you pay attention, you will see a few relics of the slate industry.

Just beyond the 1-mile mark, you cross the first of 18 legal agricultural crossings. While these are used only sporadically, use caution—especially if you hear farm machinery. The trail temporarily narrows to a single-track setting, but widens out again by the 2-mile mark. Here, you notice plenty of American beech trees, as well as some eastern hemlocks, which attract deer to the area.

In another half-mile, you pass through a rock cut before wetlands line the left edge of the trail for nearly half a mile. Beyond the 3.5-mile mark, you see a large pond off to the left, created by recent beaver activity. In fact, you may see some recently felled trees (or even a beaver at work) if you look carefully. A bridge just ahead offers a nice spot to rest and look for beavers.

You cross busy Route 30 at grade soon after you have traveled 4 miles. During the summer, you may see many small blue wild-flowers, known as chicory, along the trail's edge. The highway parallels the trail's left side all the way into Poultney, although most of the time it is barely visable. Farm fields outlined by low mountains make up the bucolic views on the right side.

After the 5.5-mile mark, you pass through a stand of aspen trees, often mistaken for white birch trees. Another wetland lines the trail's left side, and you may see a beaver or woodchuck in this area, which also is dotted with a mix of colorful wildflowers.

In another mile, you enter the town of Poultney, and see a small park where newly planted trees surround the trail as you approach the Poultney depot. There are several parking spaces available near the depot. You may want to stop in the town of Poultney, which maintains a small-town America atmosphere. If you are hungry or need a break, you will find a few restaurants here as well as several small shops.

As you continue on the trail, you soon cross one of the trail's longest bridges, nearly 100 feet long. The approach to the bridge is quite rough, as some large ballast was used to fill an area that had suffered flood damage.

You will know you have reached the New York border (at 9.2 miles) when you see a small, cryptic sign that says "Explosives." It is a warning that explosives are still used at a nearby active quarry, easily visible on your left side. The quarry is located in New York, and while the corridor appears open for some distance, it is technically not open for trail use at this time. The southern section of Vermont's Delaware and Hudson Trail resumes about 15 miles south of Poultney (see next page for details).

32. Delaware and Hudson Rail Trail (Southern Section)

Endpoints: West Pawlet to West Rupert

Location: Rutland and Bennington Counties

Length: 10.6 miles

Surface: Original ballast, ranging from hard-packed cinder to gravel

Uses:

Contact: Gary Salmon, Trails Coordinator
Department of Forests, Parks and Recreation
Vermont Agency of Natural Resources
RR 2, Box 2161
Pittsford, VT 05763
802-483-2314

◆ ◆ ◆

I f you thought the northern section of the Delaware and Hudson Rail Trail (page 203) was scenic, just wait until you get onto the southern section! Fields of corn mix with meadows of wildflowers along the lightly wooded trail that makes up the second half of the currently existing D&H Trail. The State of New York owns the undeveloped section between the two Vermont sections, and it is unclear when it will open to create a continuous 34.3-mile trail.

To get to the northern terminus of the D&H's southern section, take State Route 30 south from U.S. Route 4 through Poultney. About 11 miles south of Poultney, you want to veer right onto route 153, where a sign indicates that you are 3 miles from West Pawlet. As you approach the town, you will see obvious signs of the slate industry, including huge piles of slate. When the road comes to a

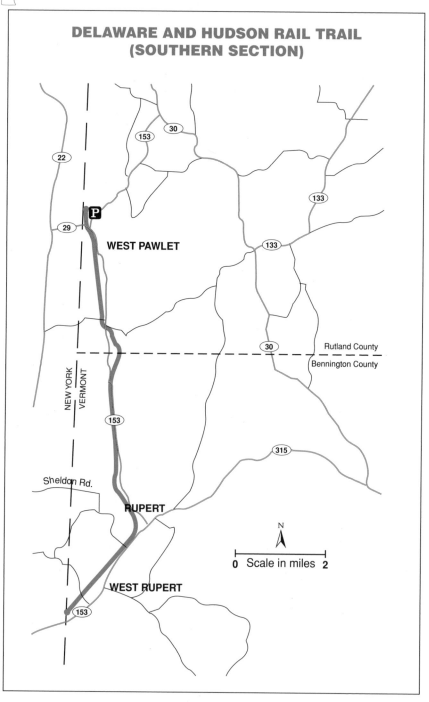

DELAWARE AND HUDSON RAIL TRAIL
(SOUTHERN SECTION)

22

153   30

P

29

WEST PAWLET

133

133

30   Rutland County
Bennington County

NEW YORK   VERMONT

153

315

Sheldon Rd.

RUPERT

N

0   Scale in miles   2

WEST RUPERT

153

T, turn right, and the rail corridor will be immediately on your right, alongside a depot. You can park in the small gravel lot next to the depot.

You are now just inside the Vermont border, and you want to head left on the trail, immediately crossing over this section's longest bridge. Within a half-mile, you will get some views of the stunning Vermont scenery, particularly off to your right. At your side are vast fields of corn, which give way to rolling hillsides, only to be overtaken by much steeper mountains.

The trail generally parallels Route 153 (on the left) for most of its length, but the rural landscapes on the right keep your eyes happily occupied. You actually cross Route 153 about 2.5-miles from West Pawlet. Although the trail is wooded in this area, you begin getting glimpses of the Indian River on your right. You cross Route 153 again at the 4-mile mark. Use caution here as the trail crosses the road in a fairly blind spot, and motorists have no warning of a trail crossing.

On the other side of Route 153, the trail resumes its tree-lined route. You continue to parallel mountains on the right, while corn fields alternate with fallow fields on the left. Within a little more than 2 miles you head into the town of Rupert, with wonderful

An occasional break in the trees reveals a view to a nearby farm.

mountain vistas in every direction. You cross a couple of streets as you pass through this tiny hamlet (which offers no services) and cross a short bridge leaving town.

Beyond the town, views from the trail become even more spectacular. Corn stalks are about the only vegetation surrounding the corridor, thus providing you with panoramic mountain scenery. Route 153 runs close by the trail for about a mile until the trail begins veering to the right. At this point, you see the town of West Rupert, although the trail only skirts its edges.

After crossing Hebron Cross Road, the trail continues about another half-mile to the New York border, passing through farmland for the remaining distance. When the trail reaches Route 153 again, you will know you are in New York. The corridor ahead gets progressively more overgrown and the bridges are impassable. It is uncertain whether or not this section of the former rail corridor will be converted into a trail.

33. Montpelier and Wells River Trail

Endpoints: Ricker Pond (in Groton State Forest) to Marshfield

Location: Caledonia County

Length: 14.5 miles

Surface: Original ballast, ranging from sand to a mix of coarse gravel and dirt

Uses:

Contact: David Willard
Trails Coordinator
Vermont Agency of Natural Resources
Department of Forests, Parks and Recreation
184 Portland Street
St. Johnsbury, VT 05819
802-748-8787

◆◆◆

The area that now makes up Vermont's Groton State Forest has a long history, beginning with the Abenaki Indians who are believed to have camped and hunted there. Later, explorers moved through the region, with the first white settlers arriving after the Revolutionary War. The land was deemed too rugged for farming but ideal for logging. It didn't take long for several mills to begin operating in a town named Groton.

By 1873, the Montpelier and Wells River Railroad had opened to serve the mills and to provide a connection between the Central Vermont and the Boston & Maine Railroads. The Montpelier and Wells also brought passengers to the area, many seeking places to camp and swim along the scenic shores of Lake Groton.

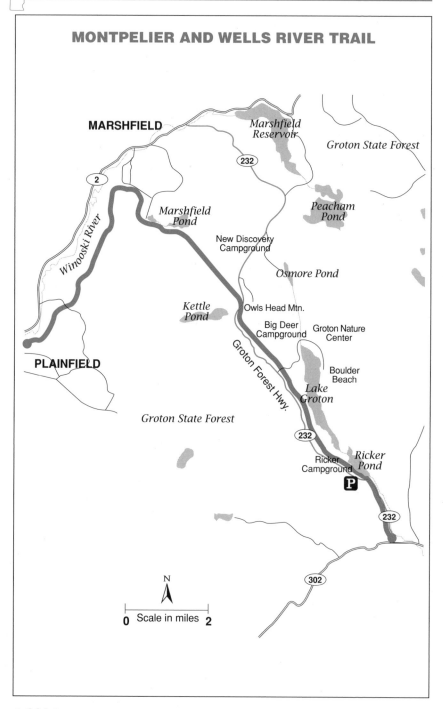

MONTPELIER AND WELLS RIVER TRAIL

MARSHFIELD

Marshfield Reservoir

Groton State Forest

232

2

Winooski River

Marshfield Pond

Peacham Pond

New Discovery Campground

Osmore Pond

Kettle Pond

Owls Head Mtn.

Big Deer Campground

Groton Nature Center

Groton Forest Hwy.

Boulder Beach

Lake Groton

PLAINFIELD

Groton State Forest

232

Ricker Pond

Ricker Campground

P

232

302

N

0 Scale in miles 2

The sheer granite cliffs of Owl's Head Mountain command your attention in the trail's mid-section.

Virtually every virgin tree in the area was logged by the 1920s, although the rail line remained in service until 1956. The Groton State Forest is now Vermont's second largest contiguous landholding at 25,000 acres. As the area revegetates, the land is selectively logged and is used extensively for recreational purposes.

To get to the southern end of the trail, take U.S. Route 302 west from Groton to Route 232 (Groton Forest Highway) north. Travel 1.6 miles north to a parking lot near Ricker Pond on the right side of the road. Park here, and plan to head north after taking in some views of Ricker Pond. The trail technically continues back to Route 302 (on the opposite side of 232), but offers little scenery.

This parking lot was originally home to one of the nation's longest continuously running sawmills, operating from 1857 to 1963. As you begin the trail, the surface is a mix of sand and gravel, with occasional sharp rocks protruding through the surface.

Within 0.3 miles, you pass through a gate, signaling your entrance into the Ricker Campground. Here, you pass about 30 tent sites and several lean-to's, as well as rest rooms and drinking water. When you get to a fork in the trail, you want to stay to the right—the left fork takes you to the camping registration area and an alternate parking lot for the trail. You leave the campground through a second gate.

Just after 1 mile, you pass by the Depot Brook Trail and an informational kiosk that outlines many of the area's snowmobiling trails. By the 2-mile mark, you cross over a second dirt road that leads to a new lakefront development. The trail is lined on both sides with a young forest of maple, beech and oak, with occasional aspen and white pine trees.

Within a half-mile, you begin picking up views of Lake Groton on your right, while a rocky embankment lines your left side. You continue gradually ascending, as you have been since the trail's start, but the surface gets more rough in this section. After 3 miles, you see a "Scenic View" sign on your left that leads you up to a higher point for better lake viewing.

In another half-mile, you reach a paved road that leads to the Big Deer and Stillwater Campgrounds, a nature center, picnic tables and Boulder Beach—a pleasant side trip. If you take the road to the right, within 2 miles (mostly downhill) you reach Boulder Beach, where picnic tables abound in a wonderfully scenic setting along the shores of Lake Groton.

Once back on the trail, you pass the former site of Peabody's Mill off to the right. About 5 miles into your journey, you cross over a small bridge as you continue climbing gradually uphill. Soon you cross another paved road, which is the main forest road (Route 232), and the views open up dramatically to the towering mountains on your right.

Douglas fir trees line the trail's left side and a wetland parallels the right side, before a mix of deciduous and evergreen trees again overtake the corridor. By mile 6, the forest canopy again opens up, offering spectacular views of the sheer granite cliffs of Owl's Head Mountain on the right. You can reach the top of Owl's Head thanks to the members of the Civilian Conservation Corps, who built the road to the right and the short trail leading to the top. From this lofty vantage point, you literally get a "bird's eye" view of the lakes and forest, with the trail running straight through the middle.

Back on the rail-trail, you soon cross a lightly-traveled road at grade. Goldenrod, milkweeds and a mix of wild daisies now accent the trail's perimeter, while patches of wetlands dot the

Karen-Lee Ryan

The wide surface of the Montpelier and Wells Trail provides ample room for everyone to enjoy the trail.

surrounding landscape. Occasional large boulders poke through the trail's rutted surface in the vicinity of mile 7. Beyond this point, trees again begin to shroud the trail, which temporarily narrows.

You will soon see views of Marshfield Pond. By the 8-mile mark, the surface has improved significantly, and the mountain views are spectacular. Be sure to look to your right—and even behind you—to catch the panoramic views. As you continue, the surface alternates between quite rough and not-so-rough.

Just less than 9 miles from Ricker Pond, you arrive at another fork. The branch to the right (where you will see a 35 mile-per-hour sign posted) is a road, while the former railroad corridor continues on the left branch. The trail gets a bit sandy in this section, which seems more lightly used than earlier sections of the trail. Trees form a canopy overhead, with dense forest off to the left, and an occasional clearing on the right.

At about 9.5 miles, you reach yet another fork, and the trail again continues on the left branch. You will find a gate here; all recreational users are welcome to proceed along the trail. (The gate was put up to prevent people from driving cars and camping along the corridor.)

The trail continues for more than 3 miles, curving west and then southwest for its remaining distance. You will pass several clearings and logging roads as you wend your way toward the Winooski River. The trail ends before reaching the Winooski River, which you may hear off to your right.

New Hampshire's Great Rail-Trails

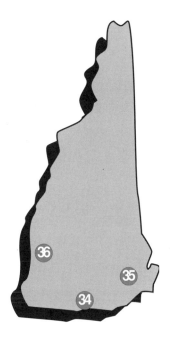

34. Mason Railroad Trail
35. Rockingham Recreational Trail
36. Sugar River Trail

Pratt Pond may be the scenic highlight of the Mason Railroad Trail.

34. Mason Railroad Trail

Endpoints:	Mason Township, between the Massachusetts border and the Wilton Township border
Location:	Hillsborough County
Length:	7 miles
Surface:	Original ballast mixed with sand and some larger rocks
Uses:	
Contact:	Liz Fletcher, Commissioner Mason Conservation Commission Mann House Darling Hill Road Mason, NH 03048 603-878-2070

◆ ◆ ◆

Based on the sandy surface that makes up much of the Mason Railroad Trail, you might think your destination would be the ocean, not land-locked Pratt Pond. On the way to this scenic destination, the lightly-traveled Mason Railroad Trail passes through wonderful lowland forests, while skirting a mix of marshes and cutting through several granite outcroppings.

The original railroad line, which later became a branch of the Boston & Maine Railroad, served the granite industry in southern New Hampshire. Passengers also used the line. In fact, local lore maintains that Henry David Thoreau rode this line on his climb to Mt. Monadnock in the 1800s. Business on the line waned in the late 1950s, although the line was not officially abandoned until the late 1970s.

To get to the trail from Interstate 495, take Route 119 north-west to Townsend, Massachusetts. Continue west toward West

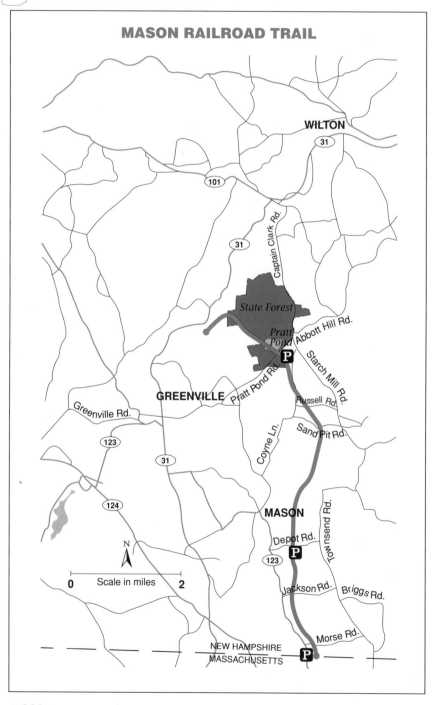

MASON RAILROAD TRAIL

Townsend for less than 2 miles, veering right at a sign that points toward Mason, New Hampshire, and another that reads "Greenville 8." In 1.5 miles, veer right at the fork and proceed 1 mile to the Massachusetts/New Hampshire border. A gravel trail parking lot is located on the left side of the road. To get onto the trail, take a right on Morse Road (which is just up the road ahead of you) and travel uphill for 0.3 miles. You will see an orange gate on the trail corridor to the left, which is the direction you want to travel. If you head right, the trail ends in less than a half-mile at the state line because the tracks are still in place in Massachusetts.

As you begin the trail, look to your right to catch a glimpse of a small waterfall before you curve gradually into the woods. An occasional railroad tie crosses the trail and sporadic rocks jut through the surface. You are quickly surrounded by a lush forest of pine, oak and maple, with birch trees randomly thrown into the mix. Rocky embankments, often covered with wild ferns, line both sides of the trail.

You head slightly uphill beyond the 1-mile mark as the surface becomes more hard-packed, and you cross over Jackson Street on a high bridge at approximately 1.5 miles. Scores of large stone blocks support the bridge, which you can see if you stop on the bridge for a careful look. Once across the bridge, the surface has some erosion problems, so use caution.

After passing a couple of homes, you cross Depot Road in another half-mile. While no remnants of the depot remain, the building most likely sat on the right side of the corridor, which is now a parking area for the trail. As you continue uphill for the next couple of miles, the trail gets progressively wider. Some relics of the granite industry exist in this area, primarily in the form of granite slabs in the trail's vicinity.

Fragrant pines and fir trees line the trail's right side, while oaks shroud most of the rocky mounds on the left, as you approach Sand Pit Road more than 4 miles from the start of the trail. If you take a left on this road, you will skirt the edge of a quarry for about a half-mile before arriving at a small community park with a portable toilet.

Sand Pit Road is aptly named, for after crossing the road, the trail gets quite sandy and begins to narrow. A railroad bridge is missing here, and a sandy fill, coupled with a tiny footbridge, carry

Karen-Lee Ryan

Mountain bicyclists enjoy the rugged surface of the Mason Railroad Trail.

you over side-by-side ponds connected by a creek. You go down a sandy hill to cross another bridge (with wide spaces between the planks) before going up an even sandier bank after which the trail levels out and crosses Russell Road. You might want to take a break at the edge of the ponds to watch the birds who are drawn to the area.

The trail continues its straight path on the other side of Russell Road and mature trees hover over the trail. Around the trail's 5-mile mark, you cross Wilton Avenue and parallel it for about a half-mile. You continue an uphill climb, and after you cross under a set of power lines, the trail veers away from the road. At this point, state forest land lines the left side.

Near mile 6, you reach the highlight of the trail, Pratt Pond, just beyond Pratt Pond Road, where parking is available. Jagged rock formations outline the edge of the pond above pockets of white pine trees interspersed with the occasional maple. In the summer, many wildflowers bloom here, and later in the year the area bursts with the fall color that makes New England famous.

Pratt Pond will line your right side for about a half-mile before you return to dense woods. The state forest continues, now on your right, for another half-mile.

The managed section of the trail ends 7 miles from where you started, however, the corridor does continue (with a few obstructions) for another 2 miles. In this section, the trail curves west before turning south toward Greenville.

The trail ends where a massive bridge that once spanned the valley into Greenville is no longer in place. The stone supports for the railroad bridge still stand, towering almost 60 feet in the air. These structures are a striking reminder of the region's railroad heritage.

Paul Angiolillo

Volunteers help maintain the Rockingham Recreational Trail
throughout the year.

35. Rockingham Recreational Trail (Portsmouth Branch)

Endpoints: Manchester to Newfields

Location: Rockingham County

Length: 25.5 miles

Surface: Gravel and original ballast

Uses: [icons: hiking, bicycling, horseback riding, cross-country skiing, snowmobiling]

Contact: Paul Gray, Chief
Bureau of Trails
Division of Parks and Recreation
New Hampshire Department of Resources
  and Economic Development
P.O. Box 856
Concord NH 03302
603-271-3254

◆◆◆

Manchester, the largest city in New Hampshire, boasts a long, well-maintained rail-trail just outside the city limits. This 25-mile corridor, once part of the extensive Boston & Maine Railroad network, runs almost one-third of the way across the state, ending just a few miles from the Atlantic Ocean.

This section of Boston & Maine Railroad corridor, called the Portsmouth Branch, originally served the textile industry—back when Manchester's textile mills made this city the home of the textile revolution. The Portsmouth Branch of the Rockingham Recreational Trail was eventually opened to the public in 1991.

The trail, which also doubles as a corridor for a buried AT&T fiber-optic line, passes through a sparsely inhabited landscape of

ROCKINGHAM RECREATIONAL TRAIL
(PORTSMOUTH BRANCH)

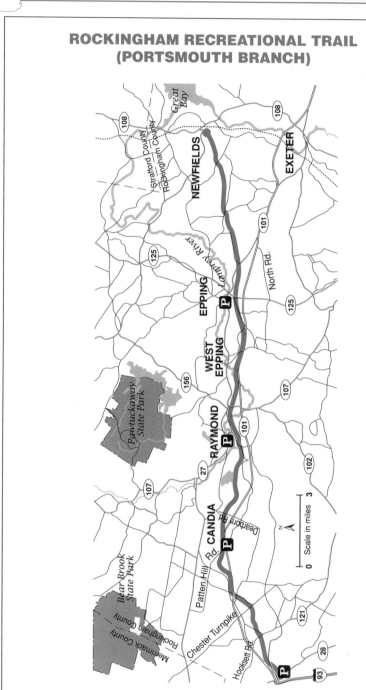

woods, fields and lakes, and several small towns. Three short tunnels lend an air of drama, and several stone walls bordering the trail add a touch of history.

Travelers should be aware that this isn't the only trail in the area known as the Rockingham Recreational Trail. A few miles south, there is a 14-mile trail of the same name running from Windham Depot to Fremont. This shorter trail is actually the original Rockingham Recreational Trail, created in the mid-1980s mainly to accommodate the growing popularity of snowmobiles, all-terrain vehicles and motorized dirt bikes. The New Hampshire Bureau of Trails currently is working to link the two Rockingham trails to each other and to a third trail to create a large triangular trail network in southeastern New Hampshire.

There are several good starting points along the 25-mile rail-trail, including convenient parking areas in Candia, Raymond and Epping. To reach the westernmost endpoint near Manchester, take Exit 7 off Interstate 93 onto Route 101 East. Almost immediately, take Exit 1 off Route 101 and go south on Route 28. Proceed around a traffic rotary and then turn into a parking lot at Lake Massabesic on the left. If the lot is full or closed, simply park at one of the turn-offs on Route 28 across from the lake.

Departing from the western terminus, the rail-trail follows the shoreline of Lake Massabesic, which is ringed by a network of popular hiking and biking trails. Trails that branch off to the right from the "Rock Rec" lead to this network of trails. If you continue another 3 miles on the rail-trail, you will reach a four-way intersection with another trail. The trail on the left climbs gradually toward Tower Hill Pond, which also offers a network of trails.

At the 5-mile mark, you reach a tunnel underneath Route 101. A half-mile farther, you approach a shorter tunnel. The landscape now settles into a quiet woods of pine, birch and oak, and remains that way for several miles. After another 4 miles, the site of the former East Candia Railroad Station will appear on the left, just before an intersection with a paved road. There is a parking area here with a sign reading "East Candia Depot." This is a good place to begin a shorter trip along the rail-trail.

Beyond the depot, the corridor becomes more secluded as it approaches Onway Lake. The trail and land near Onway Lake are privately owned, with non-motorized access permitted. Be sure to pass considerately, and respect the wishes of the local owners.

After the lake, the rail-trail takes on several interesting features. First, it runs along an elevated stretch through deep woods. Next, it passes through a granite cut. And, at mile 12, the trail enters another short tunnel. Around the trail's halfway point, you reach quaint Raymond, which is a nice place to rest and eat. You can also explore some of the handsome buildings, such as the restored railroad station, which now houses the Raymond Historical Society.

Next, you cross a large old railroad bridge. While the structure is sturdy, bikes should be walked across its widely-spaced flooring. The next intersection is a rural highway near Route 101, with a mall-like stretch of department stores. Soon the trail is back in the woods again, with the Lamprey River appearing on the right.

In the town of Epping, the trail crosses another rural highway. This is also where the original Rockingham Trail from Fremont eventually will join this trail when a bridge crossing is improved. As you continue east toward Newfields, the trail has a few bumpy and rutted spots. You soon pass by a speedway track and grandstands on the right. However, the last several miles of the trail, through Newfields, are some of its most tranquil and secluded. Take time to enjoy the peaceful setting.

The trail ends at an abandoned railroad depot, located just off Route 108, about a half-mile north of the junction with Route 85. At this point, you are just a few miles south of lively Durham, home to the sizable University of New Hampshire. Head north on Route 108 to Durham, or go south to reach the town of Exeter, where you'll find one of the country's oldest and most prestigious private schools, Phillips Exeter Academy.

36. Sugar River Trail

Endpoints: Newport to Claremont

Location: Sullivan County

Length: 10 miles

Surface: Gravel and original ballast

Uses:

Contact: Bob Spoerl, Program Specialist
Bureau of Trails
Division of Parks and Recreation
New Hampshire Department of Resources
    and Economic Development
P.O. Box 1856
Concord, NH 03302
603-271-3254

◆◆◆

True to its name, the Sugar River Trail offers the unhurried traveler a sweet place to linger. You'll also have plenty of opportunities to enjoy the water on this 10-mile trail that hugs the river's wooded shores and crosses the river and its feeder streams on almost a dozen bridges. You'll encounter sturdy iron truss and girder bridges and small wooden ones, as well as the trail's two masterpieces: a pair of huge covered bridges, built by master woodworkers a century ago to carry trains from Newport to Claremont.

Like many railroads in New Hampshire, the Boston & Maine Railroad line from Concord to Claremont (completed in 1872) closed down in the 1960s, after losing much of its business to highways. A small company bought the 10-mile stretch from Newport to Claremont, however, and kept it running until 1977.

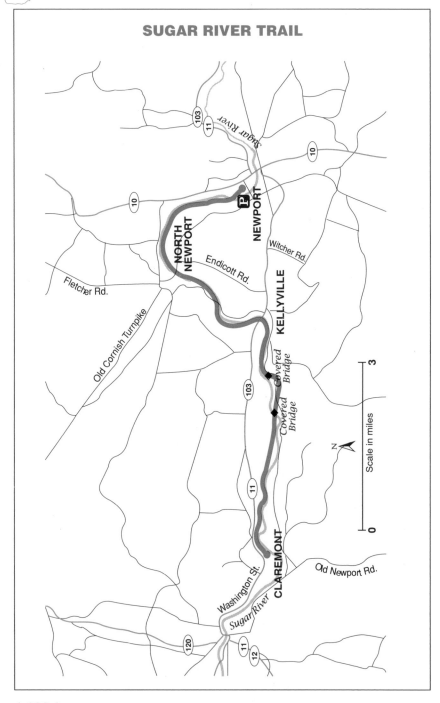

SUGAR RIVER TRAIL

Today, the corridor offers various trail users a good place to escape from the busy world. The easily accessible Sugar River Trail is shady in the summer and lined with packed snow in the winter (from skiers and snowmobilers), making it a pleasant excursion at any time of the year.

You can begin the trail in Newport, which is in the vicinity of Mt. Sunapee and Pillsbury State Parks. Mt. Sunapee offers a swimming beach and a ski mountain, where the ski trails are open for hiking in the summer. In early August, the Park hosts the state's most popular crafts festival. Less-developed Pillsbury State Park offers camping, hiking and mountain-biking. The town of Newport has an attractive brick opera house, where plays and musical performances are held. You'll also find a large town green (with a gazebo), and a restored railroad depot.

You can get to the Newport trailhead from Interstate 89. Take Exit 9 to Route 103, and head west, passing the towns of Bradford and Newbury, and Sunapee Lake before entering Newport. Head north on Route 10 for a quarter-mile past the town green, and turn left onto Belknap Avenue. A well-marked parking lot is located ahead on the right.

Traveling west out of Newport, the rail-trail passes backyards and an open field, before crossing the Sugar River at a small truss bridge. Then, after crossing a road, you might see some shaggy Scotch Highland cattle in a field on the left. The surface may be sandy in places; this is the softest part of the trail. If you look carefully into the woods on the right, you'll see three T-shaped stones and a 5-foot pillar. These are the remnants of a "rail rest," a structure once used for storing the extra rails needed to repair the track.

Two miles from Newport, the Sugar River makes its northern-most bend and widens as the river is joined by its northern branch. This river flows all the way to the Connecticut River, a few miles west of Claremont.

At this point, the trail's landscape becomes wooded with hemlock, pine and a mix of hardwood trees surrounding the route. The river courses below you in a ravine. In another half-mile, you reach the first major bridge, an iron truss bridge. The remains of an old mill are visible down the river to the left. Once over this first bridge, you almost immediately cross another. This one is made out of large iron plates, or girders, rather than trusses. These two bridges illustrate that when various engineers were involved in creating this railroad line, each one had his own specialty. Three more small bridges follow.

At the 5-mile mark (the trail's halfway point) you pass underneath the Route 11/103 bridge. The bridge is slated for reconstruction in 1996, which will result in a detour.

A mile later, you encounter the trail's first covered bridge. This is a good place to stop and relax. The handsome lattice work of this truss bridge wasn't merely decorative, but an ingenious engineering design for shifting the weight of a 100-ton train from truss to truss. The two covered bridges on the Sugar River Trail may be two of only a handful of remaining covered railroad bridges in the United States. An added benefit is that, unlike most covered bridges in New England, this one has no motorized traffic on it. You can stop here to inspect the bridge and enjoy the sights for as long as you want.

At about the 6.5-mile mark, a dirt road joins the rail-trail for about a quarter-mile, before veering off again into the woods on the right. After another mile, the second covered bridge appears. It's slightly smaller—only about 130 feet long—but still interesting. Soon, the trail begins to parallel Route 11/103 on the right, eventually ending at an orange gate along the highway.

The state is planning to build a parking lot on Route 11/103 just before this pull-off. A half-mile or so further along Route 103 from the trail's end is a large shopping center on the outskirts of Claremont. If you decide to continue into Claremont, you will be rewarded with some classic New England architecture. You will also find a number of eateries, including a time-honored diner. If you haven't had enough outside adventure for one day, you can continue about 10 miles north to Mt. Ascutney in Vermont, which is a haven for hikers.

Paul Angiolillo

The Sugar River Trail's covered railroad bridges offer a quintessential New England experience.

Maine's Great Rail-Trails

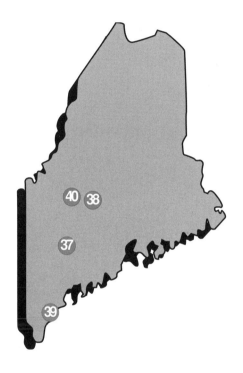

37. Jay to Farmington Trail
38. Solon to Bingham Trail
39. South Portland Greenbelt
40. Woodabogan Trail

Karen-Lee Ryan

A waterfall in Wilson Stream makes an attractive backdrop to the trail in East Wilton.

37. Jay to Farmington Trail

Endpoints: Jay to Farmington

Location: Franklin County

Length: 14.5 miles

Surface: Gravel, sand and cinder

Uses:

Contact: Scott Ramsey, Supervisor
Off-Road Vehicle Division
Bureau of Parks and Lands
Department of Conservation, Station 22
Augusta, ME 04333
207-287-4957

◆◆◆

eveloped primarily as a route for snowmobilers and off-road vehicle enthusiasts, the Jay to Farmington Trail also appeals to hikers and mountain bicyclists with a rugged spirit. The trail's sandy and often rutted surface, as well as the dense pine forest that surrounds much of the route, demand your attention. If you are not in a hurry, you can enjoy the scenery without letting the surface jostle you—physically or mentally.

This line orginally belonged to the Maine Central Railroad and served many manufacturing plants in the area. The corridor came under the management of the Maine Department of Conservation in 1982, after snowmobile riders around the state showed a strong interest in the corridor. The trail is now used by a wide range of users.

To get to the trailhead in Jay, take State Route 4 north nearly 35 miles from Interstate 495 through the town of Livermore Falls. You will soon see the Town of Jay Municipal Building on your right.

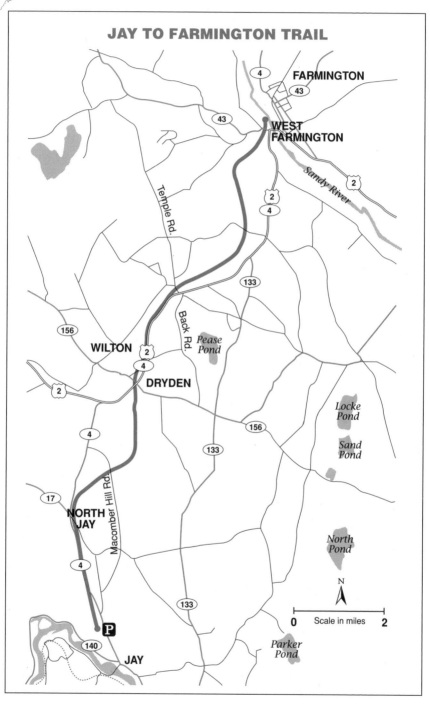

JAY TO FARMINGTON TRAIL

In a half mile, turn left (on Old Jay Road) just past the Knights of Columbus building. After passing by an auto body shop, you cross the trail corridor before arriving at a small park, where parking is available.

As you head north on the trail (the same direction that you were traveling on Route 4), the surroundings are pleasantly wooded. Within a half-mile, you arrive at the Jay depot, where a couple of different businesses have been housed in the past few years. Immediately past the depot, you cross well-traveled Route 4 at grade, so use caution. The surprisingly wide trail surface is quite sandy in this early section of the trail, which passes by a pond and behind some homes.

Soon you begin ascending on a rutted and sandy surface, which can be quite taxing. You level out past the 2-mile mark, and overall, the trail seems to improve at this point. Your surroundings get somewhat marshy and the wetland views to the right are particularly appealing. The moisture here provides a breeding ground for mosquitoes that are overly abundant in this area.

By the time you reach the 4-mile point, you are closely paralleling Route 4 and mountains fill the landscape ahead of you and to the left. On your right, you also see a massive retaining wall composed of granite blocks. Formerly the site of the North Jay rail yard, this wall lines the corridor for several hundred feet. A picnic table sits in a clearing, still within the border of the old rail yard. You resume an uphill climb as you pass by the community of North Jay.

The surface is intermittently hard-packed cinder and loose, soft sand. The fragrant smell of pine lingers in the air, while aspen trees quake at the slightest breeze. Still climbing, you cross Old Jay Road, and soon you can see two steeples and a sea of rooftops in the town below you. Just prior to 5 miles, you cross Macomber Hill Road, where an area has been cleared for some new development.

White pine and a mix of fir trees dominate the route on either side of a long rock cut. Mosses and ferns cover much of the craggy rocks, while pine trees grow out from the top of the rocky formation. The surface turns to a deep sand on the other side of the cut, although the forested setting helps keep your mind off the surface. Looking around at the nearby mountains, which once seemed to tower high above, you realize how high you've climbed.

Wetlands again approach the trail beyond 6 miles. Much of this marshy area has been created from extensive beaver activity in the area. Beyond the 7.5-mile mark, you cross four-lane Route 4 (also Route 2) at grade in the town of Wilton, followed shortly by State Route 156. Wilton is the trail's mid-point and the one of the few places to stop before Farmington. A gas station and a couple of small establishments offer limited food and supplies.

If you happen to see a "No Trespassing Without a Permit" sign, don't worry; the sign is aimed only at the automobiles that once used the route. The trail narrows out for a stretch beyond Wilton, while the surface deteriorates into rutted sand. A bridge soon carries you across Wilson Stream, which ripples next to the trail by mile 9. Route 4 continues along your right side for a couple of miles, and just before mile 10 you get a short stretch of hard-packed cinder—a welcome respite from the sand.

Beyond mile 10, you arrive at a curved bridge that spans a main road through East Wilton, as well as Wilson Stream. Built by Western Maine ATV Association and Woodland Wanderers Snowmobile Club, this bridge is designed for one-way snowmobile or off-road-vehicle traffic. Use caution on the bridge if other trail users are nearby. The bridge offers sweeping views of the surrounding landscape, as well as a waterfall in Wilson Stream to the left. A pizza restaurant sits adjacent to the trail just beyond the bridge—the last stop before Farmington.

You are back into a dense pine forest, mixed with aspen and oak, after the 11-mile mark. The surface continues alternating between sand and cinder. While you may feel a million miles away from anywhere, civilization is close by on Route 4. At times, you will see small signs for shops and restaurants. These are provided for the benefit of snowmobilers who travel long distances and may not know when to venture off the trail.

The next couple of miles continue to feel quite remote and wooded. You can almost envision an encounter with a deer, a bear or a moose on this stretch of path, but that would be very unlikely. The surface has some chunky spots as you pass through wetlands near mile 13.

Beyond mile 14, you cross Hardy Stream on the trail's second longest bridge. At this point, you get your first glimpses into West Farmington in the distance. Within a half-mile, you reach State

One of the trail's two long wooden bridges spans Wilson Stream in the town of East Wilton.

Route 43 after passing by the building of an oil company that was once served by the railroad. At this point, you are a half-mile from the trail's end at Sandy River. If you continue straight on the corridor, you will soon see the expansive river ahead of you and some stonework that once supported a bridge into Farmington. This is a peaceful spot to stop and rest before venturing into Farmington.

Home to the University of Maine, Farmington is well worth extending your journey another mile. To get into town, go back to Route 43, turn left, and you will almost immediately see signs for Routes 4 and 2. Turn left onto the state routes and continue about a mile to Main Street. Downtown is on your left, where you find several restaurants, shops and banks, as well as a bike shop and an ice cream shop. The university is to the right and splendid Victorian architecture is scattered throughout the town. The town offers a friendly welcome back to civilization.

38. Solon to Bingham Trail

Endpoints: Solon to Bingham

Location: Somerset County

Length: 7 miles

Surface: Crushed limestone

Uses:

Contact: Frank Higgins, President
Kennebec Valley Trails, Inc.
P.O. Box 506
Bingham, ME 04920
207-672-3702

◆◆◆

Tucked along the edge of the wide Kennebec River, the Solon to Bingham Trail offers a pleasant diversion from Interstate 95. Less than 45 minutes away from the highway, this flat and scenic trail is ideal for families.

This line originated as a narrow gauge logging railroad that ran between Anson and Rockwood, Maine, although portions of the line were used by tourists early in this century. When the logging eventually ceased, Central Maine Power acquired much of the corridor. In recent years, a group called Kennebec Valley Trails, has been working to promote the corridor between Solon and Bingham as a multi-use trail. The group's ultimate goal is to create a continuous water- and land-based trail from Belgrade (just north of Augusta) to the Canadian border—all along the Kennebec River. Currently, the Solon to Bingham Trail is the cornerstone of that effort.

To get to the southern end of the trail, take Exit 36 from Interstate 95. Travel north on U.S. Route 201 for more than 20 miles into Solon. To reach the trailhead, turn left on Falls Road 0.8 miles

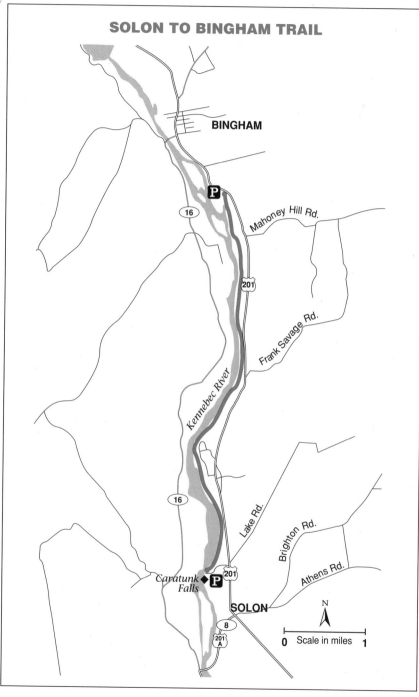

SOLON TO BINGHAM TRAIL

BINGHAM

Mahoney Hill Rd.

16

201

Frank Savage Rd.

Kennebec River

16

Lake Rd.

Brighton Rd.

Athens Rd.

Caratunk Falls

201

SOLON

8

201A

N

0 Scale in miles 1

The wide **Kennebec River** dominates the setting of the **Solon** to **Bingham** Trail.

north of the intersection of U.S. 201 and State Route 8; go downhill and veer right to reach the boat launch and trail parking area. The trail, which almost seems like a continuation of the road, will be directly in front of you paralleling the river. (If you want to view the huge dam that creates the Caratunk Falls and a massive railroad trestle overhead, continue straight on Falls Road before parking.)

As you begin the trail, the wide Kennebec River captivates you, while the smooth surface allows your attention to focus on the river. The trail carves along the edge of the river for the first couple of miles. Mountain bluffs rise up along the river's western edge, while a mix of hardwoods—including aspen, birch, oak, maple and pine—skirt the right side of the trail.

In less than a mile, you may become aware that Route 201 is running parallel to the trail. The trail is sunken down next to the river, and the highway is significantly above your right side, so you may barely notice it. Soon the trail takes on the feel of an island, as water surrounds both sides of the path for more than a half-mile. As the river and trail veer away from the highway, you pass by a residential enclave.

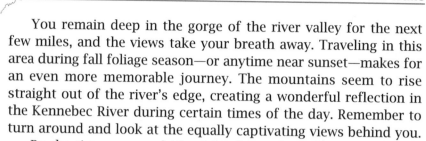

You remain deep in the gorge of the river valley for the next few miles, and the views take your breath away. Traveling in this area during fall foliage season—or anytime near sunset—makes for an even more memorable journey. The mountains seem to rise straight out of the river's edge, creating a wonderful reflection in the Kennebec River during certain times of the day. Remember to turn around and look at the equally captivating views behind you.

By the time you reach the 4.5-mile mark, a thin band of trees begins to separate you from the river. In less 2 miles, the trail veers more to the right—away from the river—eventually turning toward U.S. Route 201. A small footbridge signals that you are close to the trail's end. Soon, you reach Route 201, and if you travel left on the highway, you will reach a whitewater rafting information center.

If you plan ahead, you could combine your favorite land-based recreational activity with a fun-filled water-based one. Some people also park here and travel downriver toward Solon.

39. South Portland Greenbelt

Endpoints: Elm Street to Stanford Street in South Portland

Location: Cumberland County

Length: 2 miles (will be 4 miles when completed)

Surface: Asphalt

Uses:

Contact: Tex Haeuser
Planning Director
City Hall
25 Cottage Road
South Portland, ME 04106
207-767-3201

Across the harbor from downtown Portland, this tiny gem of a trail offers stunning views of Maine's largest city, while providing a flavor of the water-based industries that fuel this New England port city.

The line that is now the South Portland Greenbelt began as part of a short line railroad known as the Portland Terminal Company. It primarily served the oil industry, which has numerous oil storage tanks lining the watery perimeter of South Portland. Guilford Trans-portation took over the short line operation in the early 1980s and abandoned this line soon thereafter. The first 2 miles of the trail were dedicated in 1989.

To get to the South Portland Greenbelt, take Exit 7 from the Maine Turnpike (Interstate 95). After the toll booth, take the second right onto Broadway. Within 2 miles you cross Route 1; be sure to continue straight on Broadway. In just over a mile, turn left onto Elm Street. You can pick up the trail at the end of Pearl Street. There

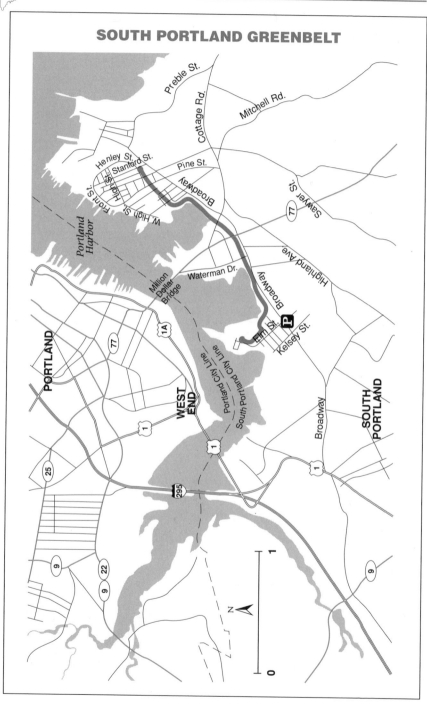

SOUTH PORTLAND GREENBELT

is no designated parking, so find a legal space on one of the side streets, or park on Broadway near Elm.

From the end of Pearl Street, go right on the trail; if you go left, the trail ends at a set of railroad tracks within a couple of blocks. Immediately upon getting onto the asphalt path, you see Portland's West End on the opposite bank of the Fore River. A residential area lines the right side, and you are likely to see many local residents walking, skating or bicycling on the trail. The trail traverses most of South Portland, and many people use the trail as a transportation thoroughfare.

In less than a half-mile, you cross a bridge and pass the local fire station, bringing you parallel to Broadway. Several shopping plazas are located near busy Hanson Street, where you cross the road at-grade. This is the start of the several-block downtown area of South Portland. In another 0.3 miles, you reach State Route 77, which is Ocean Street through town. If you turn left, you

Karen-Lee Ryan

Dusk sets in over the Portland Skyline.

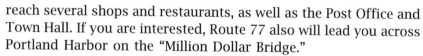

reach several shops and restaurants, as well as the Post Office and Town Hall. If you are interested, Route 77 also will lead you across Portland Harbor on the "Million Dollar Bridge."

As soon as you cross Ocean Street, you skirt the edge of the South Portland Rose Garden, filled with roses of every color. A gazebo, a large fountain and a small foot bridge over a creek give the park a days-gone-by feeling. Take some time to enjoy this pleasant community resource.

After crossing busy Cottage Street at grade, where a trail dedication marker is located, the views to the left open up again, highlighting the Portland skyline. This panoramic view is particularly dramatic at sunset. On your right, residential neighborhoods have resumed and continue beyond the 1.5-mile mark. After two quick road crossings, the land to your left turns into a meadow with colorful wildflowers. Baseball fields sit adjacent to the trail's right side.

The trail briefly travels on Maple Road at 1.7 miles. The surface is bumpy in this area, caused by railroad ties that are still in place under the pavement. You pass a community center with a basketball court just before the trail ends at the 2-mile mark at Stanford Street. A large fence blocks any further travel on the route, where inactive railroad tracks are still in place. A sidewalk on Henley Street curves around toward the water, but does not really lead anywhere.

The future holds great promise for the South Portland Greenbelt. Funding has already been approved for a 2-mile eastern extension that would end at "Bug Light"—the lighthouse at the entrance of Portland Harbor. City planners also hope to get funding for an additional 3-mile extension to the west.

40. Woodabogan Trail

Endpoints: Carrabassett Valley Township between Valley Crossing and Bigelow Station

Location: Franklin County

Length: 7 miles

Surface: Original ballast and gravel

Uses:

(Skiers need to purchase a trail-use permit at the Sugarloaf/USA Touring Center before using the trail.)

Contact: Buzz Davis, Manager
Sugarloaf/USA Touring Center
RR 1, Box 5000
Carrabassett Valley, ME 04947-9799
207-237-2000

◆◆◆

Located just off the peaks of Sugarloaf/USA ski resort, the Woodabogan Trail is a popular cross-country skiing trail throughout the winter months. It is part of a 50-mile network of cross-country trails that are managed by Sugarloaf's Ski Touring Center and cater to skiers of all abilities. In warmer months, when the crowds dissipate, much of the network is open to hikers and mountain bicyclists. The Woodabogan Trail, which parallels the rocky Carrabassett River, is sure to please any time of the year.

The trail is built on one of the Sandy River/Rangely Lakes Railroad's many narrow gauge routes that originated in Farmington. The railroad company fueled two primary industries: logging and tourism. It hauled timber and other goods to Farmington, where

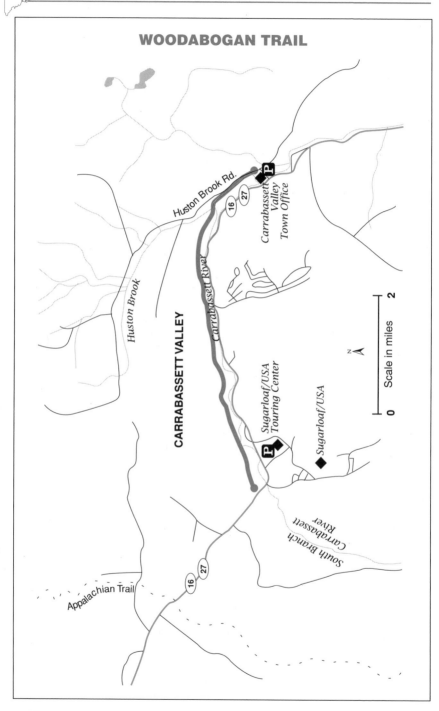

WOODABOGAN TRAIL

they would be transferred to standard railroads and transported to other destinations in the Northeast. The narrow gauge also ferried passengers to the many resort hotels lining the lakes around the town of Rangely. Both industries were already suffering at the start of the Depression, and the Sandy River/Rangely Lakes Railroad went out of business in the mid-1930s. While the corridor was used as a trail for many years, it was not until 1983 that efforts were made to improve the corridor and maintain it as a trail.

The southern end of the Woodabogan Trail is located between Kingfield and Sugarloaf/USA. To get there, take State Routes 4 and 27 north from Farmington and continue on Route 27 for about 30 miles to Kingfield. In 5 miles, you enter Carrabassett Valley and the river appears on your right. In another 4 miles, turn right when you see a small sign for the Carrabassett Valley Town Office. (This is easily missed, and if you reach the Sugarloaf information center, you will know you have gone too far.) Park at the Town Office, where you will also find picnic tables and a playground adjacent to the parking lot.

To get onto the trail, take a left onto the road from the parking lot and another left onto Huston Brook Road. (To the left is a private drive.) After passing by several small chalets, the Carrabassett River appears on your left, and you continue on the road (doubling as a trail) for about a mile. When you reach a fork, take the left branch, the official beginning of the Woodabogan Trail. The surface at the start of the trail may be the rockiest section of a fairly rugged trail surface. Sugarloaf/USA plans to smooth out the surface sometime during the summer of 1996.

After crossing over a creek and spending a few minutes enjoying the river views, you travel uphill amid a forest of oak, beech, maple, white pine, aspen and birch. These trees display a stunning array of color during the early fall months. Within a half-mile, the river comes back into view on your left, where you also catch fleeting glimpses of Route 27.

More than 2 miles from the town office, you see the first set of cascading waterfalls on the Carrabassett River. The soothing sound of rushing water not only calms your senses, but also drowns out any sounds from Route 27. Soon the trail narrows out, and the surface temporarily overflows with small boulders and stumps before smoothing out near another cascading swirl at 2.4 miles.

Wood-A-WHAT?

If you think Woodabogan seems like an unusual name for a rail-trail, you're right. Formerly called the Carrabassett River Trail, and commonly referred to as the Narrow Gauge Trail, the Woodabogan Trail acquired its latest—and most official—name as a tribute to the Penobscot Indians who once inhabited this part of Maine.

The name translates to the "toboggan trail," and it is one of dozens of trails run by the Sugarloaf/USA Touring Center with Penobscot names. If you venture onto the Center's 50-mile cross-country ski trail network, you will encounter trails with names like Gwipdez (colored leaf), Damakguay (beaver), Wezinauks (go fast) and one that you may want to avoid: Jezhawuk, which means mosquito.

By the 3-mile mark, a steep rocky wall lines your right side, and water continues to rush through the bedrock of the river. The trail begins to level out within another half-mile, although the surface continues to alternate between somewhat smooth and quite rocky. By 4.5 miles, you have veered away from the river and a marshy swampland begins to overtake the landscape on your right side. You are likely to see (or hear) pileated woodpeckers and other birds, and you may even be lucky enough to spot a moose or some deer.

Beware of an obstacle at the 5.3-mile mark, where a drainage pipe has been covered with logs. Use caution if you are not a stump jumper. A few hundred yards past these logs, a trail leads off to the left and will connect you to the Sugarloaf/USA Touring Center, and an extensive trail network.

To get to the Touring Center, head left and you soon arrive at a bridge that crosses the Carrabassett River. Even if you don't plan to go to the Touring Center, you should take this short side trip to see the spectacular river and mountain views. If you continue across the bridge to a road, briefly jog left to reach Route 27. If you look right, you see a sign for the Touring Center. The building that houses the center is about a half-mile up the access road. (You

Karen-Lee Ryan

The Carrabassett River rushes alongside much of the Woodabogan Trail.

could also park at the Touring Center and begin your journey from there.) Bike rentals are available in the summer through Sugarloaf/USA.

Back on the trail, just before the 6-mile mark, you pass an area with beaver activity. The trail, which is still on an incline, is wet in this area, with some water holes and an occasional log on the corridor. In another half-mile, you reach a gate, and if you continue a short distance farther, you arrive at the Bigelow Train Station (adjacent to Route 27). If you look to the left, you see the main entrance to the Sugarloaf/USA ski resort. The trail appears to continue on the other side of Route 27, but this is actually an access road for the Sugarloaf Golf Course.

If you turn right on Route 27, you reach the Appalachian Trail in 2 miles. This famous backcountry hiking trail continues all the way to Georgia. If you are turning around and retracing your steps, have fun—and use some caution—as the trail will have a steady decline all the way back to Valley Crossing.

Saturn Retailer Locations

For more information, please call 1-800-522-5000.

NEW YORK

Saturn of Albany
1769 Central Avenue
Albany, NY 12205
518-464-5000

Saturn of Bay Ridge
714 65th Street
Brooklyn, NY 11220
718-921-1234

Saturn of Binghamton
3612 Vestal Pky East
Vestal, NY 13850
607-797-7000

Saturn of Clarence
5535 Transit Road
Williamsville, NY 14221
716-689-8900

Saturn of Hempstead
265 N Franklin Street
Hempstead, NY 11550
516-565-2400

Saturn of Larchmont
2500 Boston Post Road
Larchmont, NY 10538
914-636-4200

Saturn of Long Island City
48-01 Northern Blvd.
Long Island City, NY 11101
718-721-1300

Saturn of Massapequa
5715 Merrick Road
Massapequa, NY 11758
516-795-3300

Saturn of Mohawk Valley
5046 Commercial Drive,
Route 5A
New York MIlls, NY 13417
315-768-3821

Saturn of Route 31
3885 Route 31
Liverpool, NY 13090
315-622-0054

Saturn of Orchard Park
3559 Southwestern Blvd.
Orchard Park, NY 14127
716-667-3100

Saturn of Poughkeepsie
600 South Road, Route 9
Poughkeepsie, NY 12601
914-462-1400

Saturn of Rochester
770 Panorama Trail East
Rochester, NY 14526
716-586-6959

Saturn of Roslyn
1043 Northern Blvd.
Roslyn, NY 11576
516-365-5055

Saturn of Smithtown
726 Middle Country Road
Saint James, NY 11780
516-360-8900

Saturn of Staten Island
2556 Hylan Blvd.
Staten Island, NY 10306
718-979-8900

Saturn of Syracuse
716 W Genesee Street
Syracuse, NY 13204
315-472-0021

Saturn of Watertown
19138 US Route 11
Watertown, NY 13601
315-788-8012

Saturn of West Nyack
250 N. Route 303
West Nyack, NY 10994
914-353-4440

Saturn of West Ridge
4692 Ridge Road West
Spencerport, NY 14559
716-352-5995

Saturn of White Plains
358 Central Avenue
White Plains, NY 10606
914-761-5000

Saturn of the Hamptons
355 Hampton Road
Southampton, NY 11968
516-287-5151

CONNECTICUT

Saturn of Branford
1003 W Main Street
Branford, CT 06405
203-483-3838

Saturn of Danbury
102 Federal Road
Danbury, CT 06813
203-730-5766

Saturn of Fairfield
421 Tunxis Hill Road
Fairfield, CT 06430
203-384-0006

Saturn of Hartford
99 Leibert Road
Hartford, CT 06120
 203-249-1303

Saturn of Stamford
747 Washington Blvd.
Stamford, CT 06901
203-961-8425

Saturn of Wallingford
1164 N Colony Road
Wallingford, CT 06492
203-949-7450

Saturn of Watertown
715 Straits Turnpike
Watertown, CT 06795
860-945-4755

RHODE ISLAND

Saturn of Warwick
1511 Bald Hill Road
Warwick, RI 02886
401-821-5800

MASSACHUSETTS

Saturn of Boston at
the Dedham Line
1585 VFW Parkway
Boston, MA 02132
617-325-4200

Saturn of Danvers
24 Commonwealth Avenue
Danvers, MA 01923
508-777-9200

Saturn of Dartmouth
143 Faunce Corner
N Dartmouth, MA 02747
508-993-2300

Saturn of Hadley
44 Russell Street
Hadley, MA 01035
413-584-4600

Saturn of Haverhill
915 S Main Street
Ward Hill, MA 01835
508-373-6700

Saturn of Hyannis
115 Bassett Lane
Hyannis, MA 02601
508-775-9000

Saturn of Natick
1000 Worcester Road
Natick, MA 01760
508-651-1800

Saturn of Quincy
54 Miller Street
Quincy, MA 02169
617-328-1000

Saturn of Raynham
1545 New State Highway
Raynham, MA 02767
508-880-5000

Saturn of Seekonk
189 Taunton Avenue
Seekonk, MA 02771
508-336-3322

Saturn of Springfield
603 E Columbus
Springfield, MA 01105
413-785-1311

Saturn of Worcester
70 Gold Star Boulevard
Worcester, MA 01606
508-791-8188

VERMONT

Saturn of South Burlington
1089 Shelburne Road
South Burlington, VT 05403
802-860-6600

Saturn of St. George
1333 S. Sunland Dr.
St. George, VT 84790
801-634-0900

NEW HAMPSHIRE

Saturn of Concord
Route 3A Bow Junction
Concord, NH 03301
603-226-5800

Saturn of Nashua
635 Amherst Street
Nashua, NH 03063
603-889-3030

Saturn of Portsmouth
1 Gosling Road
Portsmouth, NH 03801
603-430-9700

MAINE

Saturn of Bangor
327 Hogan Road
Bangor, ME 04401
207-945-9525

Saturn of Brunswick
118 Pleasant Street
Brunswick, ME 04011
207-721-8300

Saturn of Westbrook
1 Saunders Way
Westbrook, ME 04092
207-856-2400

How to Become a Rails-to-Trails Conservancy Member

RAILS -to- TRAILS CONSERVANCY

Rails-to-Trails Conservancy is a private, non-profit public charity, supported by the generous contributions of its members and friends —individuals and families like you. We invite you to join today.

Membership/Gift Membership Levels

Individual Membership **$18**

Supporting Membership **$25**

Patron Membership **$50**

Benefactor Membership **$100**

Advocate Membership **$500**

Trailblazer Society Membership **$1,000**

As a member of Rails-to-Trails Conservancy, you will receive the following benefits:

◆ A free subscription to our quarterly newsletter **Trailblazer.**

◆ A free copy of the **Sampler of America's Rail-Trails.**

◆ Discounts on Conservancy publications, merchandise and conferences.

◆ Additional membership benefits for Trailblazer Society members.

And, most importantly, you will get the satisfaction that comes from helping build a nationwide network of beautiful trails for all of us to enjoy for years (and generations) to come.

Why don't you become an RTC member today?
(Use the order form on page 265)

Rails-to-Trails Conservancy
Merchandise and Publications

40 Great Rail-Trails in the Mid-Atlantic

Another popular guide in RTC's "Great Rail-Trail" series of books! This 282-page guide book offers maps, descriptions and photos for Pennsylvania, New Jersey, Maryland, Virginia, West Virginia and Ohio. Size 5½ x 8½ inches. 1995. **#RG2** $14.95 (Members $12.95).

40 Great Rail-Trails in Michigan, Illinois, and Indiana

RTC's first in a series of eight regional guides! This 224-page guide book is complete with detailed maps, photographs, and descriptions of 40 of the best rail-trails in the Midwest. Size 5½ x 8½ inches. 1994. **#RG1** $14.95 (Members $12.95).

700 Great Rail-Trails: A National Directory

Our most popular publication! This directory offers information such as location, endpoints, length, surface material, contacts and allowable uses for 700 rail-trails in 48 states. **#GRT** $9.95 (Members $7.95)

Pennsylvania's Rail-Trails

This 4 x 9 inch guide fits in your pocket for easy access to detailed maps, trail highlights, and historical background on Pennsylvania's 60 rail-trails. This book covers more than 700 miles of trails throughout the Keystone State. 105 pp. 1994. **#PTG** $12.95. (Members $19.95).

RTC Water Bottle

Quench your thirst with this six-panel design water bottle! This colorful, heavy-duty water bottle holds 28 ounces and the exciting colors match the RTC T-shirt. **#WBBN** $4.95 (Members $3.95)

RTC short-sleeve T-Shirt

Printed on 100% cotton, this six-panel T-shirt tells the Rails-to-Trails story in a colorful design. Made in U.S.A.. Indicate size on the order form: S, M, L, X-L). **#TSS** $16.95 (Members $12.95)

RAILS
TO
TRAILS
CONSERVANCY

ORDER FORM

Item Description	Item #	Size	Qty.	Unit Price	Total Amt.
Membership					
				Sub-total	
			DC, FL, IL, OH, MI & PA Sales Tax		
Shipping & Handling Charge (merchandise & publications ONLY)					
				TOTAL	

POSTAGE & HANDLING CHARGES:

If your merchandise total is:	Please add:
Up to $15	$4.50
$15.01–$25.00	$5.50
$25.01–$50.00	$6.50
$50.01–$75.00	$7.00
$75.01 and higher	$8.00

ORDERED BY:

Name _____

Address _____

City _____

State & Zip _____

Phone Number _____

Please check payment method:

❏ My check, payable to Rails-to-Trails Conservancy, is enclosed.

❏ Please charge my: ❏ MasterCard ❏ VISA

Card # _____ Exp. Date _____

Signature _____

Please return this form (and any payment) to: Rails-to-Trails Conservancy, Shipping Department, P.O. Box 295, Federalsburg, MD 21632-0295. Or, to order by MasterCard or VISA, use our toll-free number: 1-800-888-7747, ext. 11.

Satisfaction guaranteed!

We will ship your order within 10 days of receipt; some items may be sent separately.

Rails-to-Trails Conservancy is a non-profit charitable organization as qualified under Section 501(c)(3) of the Internal Revenue Code. Contributions are tax deductible to the extent permitted by law.

To obtain a copy of the current financial statement, annual report and state registration filed by RTC, contact RTC at 1400 Sixteenth Street, NW, Suite 300, Washington, DC 20036, 202-797-5400.

RG3

About the Author

Dan Gross

Karen-Lee Ryan is a writer and editor living in Washington, D.C. As Director of Publications for Rails-to-Trails Conservancy, she helped launch the "Great Rail-Trail" series of guidebooks. She is the author of *40 Great Rail-Trails in the Mid-Atlantic* and a contributing author and the editor of *40 Great Rail-Trails in Michigan, Illinois and Indiana.* She has three additional books to her credit, and her writing has appeared in several national magazines. She also contributes a biweekly fitness column to Gazette Newspapers in Montgomery County, Maryland.